THE
STORK
IS
DEAD

Charlie Shedd

THE STORK IS DEAD

Straight Answers to Young People's Questions about Sex

WORD BOOKS
PUBLISHER
WACO, TEXAS

A DIVISION OF
WORD, INCORPORATED

THE STORK IS DEAD
Revised Edition

First Printing, February 1983
Second Printing, May 1983

Library of Congress Catalog No. 68-56991
ISBN 0-8499-2956-3
Copyright © 1968
Charlie W. Shedd
and the
Abundance Foundation

Printed in the United States of America

To the thousands of teenagers
who read edition one of
THE STORK IS DEAD
and wrote me like this:
"Thanks for your book.
It really made me think."
And to the many more who will read edition two—
Thanks to you for being a thinker too
for being what you are—
very special!

A Word from the Publisher

The "Sex and Dating" column in *Teen* magazine draws thousands of letters. And Dr. Charlie Shedd is one of the early authors of that column. From this background came the first edition of *The Stork Is Dead.*

From the moment of its first publication this book met with an enthusiastic response. Letters poured in from young people—and some not so young—expressing appreciation for a book that talked *to* and not *at* them.

Over the years since the book was first published, letters continued to come. In fact, it was the continual demand for the kind of down-to-earth help on love, sex, and dating *The Stork Is Dead* provides that led to this new, revised edition. In the process of preparing it, we consulted a random selection of young people, asking them for feedback and suggestions.

Our young "advisors" found some words and phrases they thought were out of date and some topics they felt needed more explanation—and we have taken their suggestions into account. But on the whole the kids who read *The Stork Is Dead* this time around were excited about it. They said they wished they had read it sooner, and they wished their boyfriends and brothers and sisters could read it too.

The enthusiastic response of this group of teenagers confirmed our belief that the information and ideas presented in *The Stork Is Dead* do not "creak" with age, but are young and alive and as pertinent today as when they were first presented.

Dr. Shedd no longer writes the column for *Teen* magazine, but he stays in close touch with young people, and he receives countless invitations to speak at high schools, colleges, universities, and military bases. The reason? When we asked him for his answer, he said, "I sometimes wonder myself why a grandfather would be asked to share his thoughts with the young. But as I think about it, there might be some basic answers.

"For one thing, I believe in today's youth. I respect their ability to handle the truth honestly given. So if we can learn to listen, to respect their questions, and to talk straight without condemning, they'll listen.

"I also believe they want and need someone from another generation saying, 'Marriage can be beautiful and one way to be sure yours will be is a genuine respect for sex, starting right where you are now. So, learn all you can, live up to the very finest you are, put the "reserved" signs where they should be, and one day down there in your future you too will be able to say, "Thank you, Lord, for a wonderful marriage with all these wonderful feelings of sex at its wonderful best." ' "

Preface

This is a minister. Color him dull gray.

But before you turn him off, you might like to know who let him in.

How he got in was through this special invitation. One day the editor of *Teen* magazine called from Hollywood.

"Dr. Shedd," he began, "for a long time we have been wanting this column on sex and dating. If you'll start it off, we'll run it a couple of times to see how it goes."

How it went was like taking your finger out of a dike. Like a flood of letters from all over, from every state in the union. They came from foreign countries, from the thirteens and the nineteens, the twelve-year-olds and elevens. A lot of the early twenties wrote too. But they all had this one thing in common—they were hung up somewhere on sex.

Dozens and dozens and hundreds and hundreds of letters poured into our office. As you will see, we kept the best ones. Without identification, I'll share some of these with you right out of my files.

So, that's how this preacher got in.

That's how I happen to know what's going on in the back seats of cars. In the back rooms at parties, along lover's lane; under the moon, in broad daylight, what are they doing? I know. Up in Suzie's room when the folks aren't home—I know about that too. Down on the beach, back there in the shadows, wherever the action is, I've heard it. I can tell you some things you wouldn't believe and some you already know.

Then there is one thing I know that you don't know. I know how good mature sex *can* be in marriage. That's what I want for you. But I also know what it costs and that's why I wrote this book.

It is fourteen years since the first edition of *The Stork Is Dead*. During that period I've had the high privilege of speaking to, visiting with, counseling teens by the thousands. And I've discovered two things for sure about you.

Item one: *You have some super qualities which are ultraimportant for the future.* Sure, there are some negatives around here, but the number of quality youth I know gives me high hope for the years ahead.

Item two: *In some ways you aren't much different from teenagers fourteen years ago; maybe long before that.* Sure, you are an important individual with unique qualities. Yet the better I know you, the more I hear the same questions, same problems, same frustrations, same wonderings.

So this second edition of *The Stork Is Dead* comes with the wish that you may find here certain helps to becoming the best possible you. And of this I'm sure—the best possible you is all-important because God made you for his good.

CHARLIE W. SHEDD
Fripp Island, South Carolina
1982

Contents

I

What's Smart?

I

What's Smart?

Introduction

I don't care whether it's wrong. I want to know whether it's smart.

He was a typical American teenager—sharp, natural, straightforward. He knew I was a minister so he was out to settle this early—

> Now don't give me your old religious pitch. Hell fire and sex has had it. I'm looking for some adult who will cool his moral fever long enough to tell me, "What's smart for me."
>
> What I mean is, can you give me some good reasons why we should wait? Of course I could say I don't want to hurt her. But to be real honest, how she'll feel is only part of what's bugging me. She says she'll never regret it. But my question is, "Will I?"

That is so much like the crowd I hear from. They cut right through. They lay it on the line. In fact, I wouldn't be surprised any more about anything.

Which raises that favorite adult question: "Are today's young people worse than we were?" To which the right answer is, "Yes!" The ones who are worse are worse. But that's only half the answer. The truth is, the ones who are better are so much better. So I'll take today's crowd. If I had to choose for the future I'd favor the ones from today.

They're more alert, more honest, and they're thinking hard on some basic questions:

■ *Is* there some permanent hookup between "What's right?" and "What's smart?"

■ *Are* some things so great you have to wait for the greatest?

If I get the message, a whole generation is sending out the signal— "Hell fire and sex has had it . . . tell me, 'What's smart for me?'"

As I look over the teenagers I know; when I put my ear down to my letter file; going back to my own teen years and since; I come up with five things that look like smart sex to me.

All I ask is that you give them your own deep-think. Then you decide. After all, nobody is going to determine what's smart for you but you.

1

It's Smart to Know
What You Need to Know

From here, there, everywhere, one kind of letter keeps coming.
The theme is, "My folks never told me a thing."
Here is my favorite:

> Do you know who is the great stone face? It's my mom. Especially
> when the subject is sex, she glazes over and just gets rigid. Honest, I
> wonder how she had me.

I'm sorry that's the way it is with so many. Too bad because
home could be such a good place for sex education. But if that's
how it goes at your house, you might do some checking. Could it
be you? Some parents complain, "He won't sit still long enough"
. . . or . . . "We can't get her off the phone" . . . or . . . "We
tried and they wouldn't communicate." Do you suppose your folks
feel that way? Have they been wondering how come you don't ask
questions?

I know one boy who waited and waited. Finally he decided it
would soon be hopeless if he didn't make a move. One day he went
to his parents and said, "I do think you're smart, even if I don't
act like it. But I think you should know I need to ask somebody

some things about sex. I'd rather get it from you than some of those other places."

I know that boy. I know his mother and dad. They all agreed it was one fine day.

That's what you call "acting" rather than "reacting." It's a mature way to handle your problems, especially if they deal with sex. But, you say you *have* acted; you've really tried and it didn't work? Your folks don't have it or, if they do, they won't share it.

Maybe it is their feeling that they honestly couldn't help you. They're overly nervous about sex and they got that way from their background. Then come out of your mourning and look around. There aren't many places these days where the entire community ciphers out. Teachers, doctors, ministers, counselors, adult friends; how about them? They might be a big help *if you would only ask.* Those last five words are the key. *You're* going to have to make the first move. Nobody worth listening to will approach you with, "Hi innocent! Let me now clue you in about sex!"

Suppose you did make the first move and bombed out. I get letters complaining, "I asked these other people and they were more embarrassed than I was." Then what? Then go to the library. If you know the librarian, she might be willing to help. And if she is something left over from before the earth cooled, don't give up yet. Go right over to the index and look up "Sex." Sit in the library all day if need be and educate yourself.

But you live way out in the boondocks where there isn't any library? The nearest neighbors are fifteen miles? Nobody out here cares? There is still one more possibility. Write your congressman. Tell him you want the latest government bulletins on sex and the teenager. You may be surprised at the interest he'll take. Go ahead! It won't cost you anything more than one stamp. Your parents pay taxes. They've already paid for your share.

There are a couple of places where you better move slow. One is on the advice you get from other teenagers. It needs to be sifted. It is normal for you to think that other teens are sure to be smart. That's not necessarily so. Maybe what they know is the "how to," and not the "what for." There are a lot of distorted sex thoughts in young heads. I'd check what I get from this source.

What's Smart?

There is one more place I'd take it easy. This is in "pornography." I don't need to tell you it's all over the place. Unless you're some kind of junior saint, you know what I mean. You also know where to get it, where to hide it, and how much it takes to turn you on. With this stuff I would ration myself. There are two reasons. First: A lot of it is plain fantasy. Many of the characters who write these things are some kind of weird. They don't know thing one about sex at its best Second: Too much of this mixed up data in your head can mix you up too.

You noticed the subject here is, "It's smart to know what *you* need to know."

Question: Can a teenager know too much?

Answer: I doubt it. Most young minds have something inside which sorts and stores their knowledge. The ones I know who got into trouble are not the overinformed. They are the ones who didn't know. Or they got it wrong from wrong sources. Or somebody failed to tell them at a time when they should have been told.

So what I am saying is, "Don't let it happen to you!" There is no excuse for living in a sex vacuum.

The fact is that nobody knows what you know or what you have learned or how. But you know and this truth stands:

■ IT'S YOUR HEAD AND WHAT'S IN IT IS YOUR RESPONSIBILITY!

2

It's Smart to Aim
for Uninhibited Sex

Did you ever raise peanuts? I did. Nothing so great about that because we lived in the country. Most country boys raise something. But this was new with me, and I don't recommend it for nine-year-olds (that's how old I was at the time).

The problem is that peanuts grow underground. You hoe and water and wait. You watch the tops grow. But are there any peanuts? What if there aren't any peanuts?

So I did the worst thing you can imagine. One day when my folks weren't home, I pulled up my peanuts to see. Not bad! Some half-grown, nice shape, very promising. Of course, I packed the earth around them again and waited now with confidence.

But you know what happened. You should only dig peanuts once. When you do it more often, you shatter their nervous system. They turn out funny. They get long and flat or nubby and wide. They twist and take on the oddest shapes. Some of them rot and they die. To say the least, the whole thing was awful.

Life is like my peanut crop in so many places. Many a teenager has learned the hard way that some things can't be hurried.

So this is a good thing to remember:

What's Smart?

■ YOU MIGHT TEAR UP SOMETHING THAT NEEDS MORE TIME IF YOU GET STARTED WITH SEX TOO SOON!

When you first begin to sense these feelings it's rather awesome. There are some new urges here you've never felt. You ponder this. You wonder. Then one day you suddenly realize what you have is a mysterious magnet. You're being drawn in the direction of others and they're being drawn to you. This is exciting. It's wonderful. Nothing so fine has ever happened before.

This is why dating is so all-important to the teenager. When a girl doesn't have a chance to share herself, she gets panicky. She says, "I might as well be dead," and she means it. Something way down at the core of her wants to give and be given to.

When a boy is rejected again and again, he sinks into a blue mood. He's blue because something inside is sending up blue messages. What if he never finds someone?

This is the reason the word "together" means so much at this age. It is a deeper thing than most adults can remember. "Fun together," "going together," "being together"; these have a sound for teenagers like no other sound.

All of which is very good if it isn't overdone. You know some couples who only have eyes for each other. They are oblivious to anyone else. They look ridiculous sometimes, partly because they're missing so much. Life at this age is for expanding, for drawing the circle larger to take in more and more.

If you appreciate one person so much that you can't appreciate people; if you think this one friend is so nice that you miss the nice in others, that's bad. If you are over-relating to one individual and not to the rest of your world, this too is bad. You may be stunting your own growth.

The same thing goes for sex. If you over-focus your mind on your physical relationship with this one person, see what happens? You might miss a lot of other things you need to know about this one person. One broken-hearted girl put it this way: "I guess we used sex as a substitute for getting acquainted." She said it when she told me he had asked her for his ring back. But that's how it goes. You might give in too soon and lose the very thing you wanted.

Which leads to another thing I'd like to write on your mind in big indelible letters:

■ WHAT YOU CALL "ALL THE WAY," ISN'T!

Over and over and over I hear it. My letters are loaded with "All the Way!": "He says we'll be married some day so why not go all the way?" . . . "In our school they call you a freak if you don't go all the way!" . . . "Can you tell me why if we love each other we shouldn't go all the way?"

Yes, I can tell you! I can tell you that what you are talking about actually isn't even halfway. It isn't a fourth, or an eighth, or a thirty-second. It's not even one small percentage of what you want. What you call "all the way" sex is really only "semi-sex" and very second rate.

At its best sex is a total involvement. It is the total involvement of your whole emotional makeup with the whole emotional makeup of one other person.

There is a major fallacy abroad that sex is simply the act of inter-course. But it is so much more than that. In a very real sense sex is not just something you do. When it is right, it is something that you and the person you love are becoming together. This has its roots way down at the center of the universe permanently and forever. The truth is that "All The Way" sex at its greatest isn't free. Sex like it ought to be is only for those who will pay the price of total commitment.

Which leads to another favorite theme in my letters: "I wanna be free" . . . "Don't fence me in" . . . "Give me liberty."

But right here is one of the trickiest things life does to us. It is possible in declaring ourselves free to sentence ourselves to misery. That's why I say *aim* for uninhibited sex.

"Uninhibited" means freedom to express oneself. "Inhibited" means "any impediment to free expression." "Uninhibited" means no part of you is blocking any other part. "Inhibited" means "any physical activity imposing restraint upon another activity."

There is a beautiful verse in the Bible which says, "And they were both naked, the man and his wife, and they were not ashamed." You will recognize that as a part of the Genesis story. This is how it was meant to be in our original creation.

It is a sad fact that sex-wise there are very few uninhibited people. This includes a majority of the world's married folks. Why do so many miss it? What happens? In some cases they did what I did with my peanuts. They tore up something fine before it was ready.

"Uninhibited" is not a nice word to some people. The reason is that they are thinking of "unbridled." Unbridled carries with it a sense of violence, out of control, unruly. But "uninhibited," as we use it here, has a feeling of power constrained. It is power held back, disciplined. For what? For the right time, the right place, the right use!

That's why I say:

■ AIM FOR UNINHIBITED SEX.

Great teen sex is a goal. It is the willingness to sacrifice what you want right now to get what you want in the future.

Could this be what the ancient philosopher meant when he said, "We must let the half gods go, that the gods may arrive?"

3

It's Smart to Remember
That Kicks Have Kickbacks

If you were raised in an average home, you have some kind of inner controls. If you ever went to church or Sunday school; if you listened even one day to a teacher; if you have parents, grandparents, brothers, sisters, uncles, aunts, cousins or any other relatives; you were taught something about right and wrong. If you ever made contact with anyone who had authority over you, then you're stuck with it. You have some kind of moral flashback.

Religion calls it, "God-given conscience." They say it is part of Divine creation. Psychologists call it "Moral Orientation." They say it began the first day we heard voices. But, however we got that way, something inside serves as a personal policeman.

Because this is true the wise young mind does a retake when it hears the word "kicks" and words like it. "We're out for thrills" . . . "You'll get a kick out of it" . . . "Let's go get our jollies." These are a part of the universal teen vocabulary.

They have a real appeal. They sound like an invitation to fun and they might be. But they might not. Always the smart teenager remembers that kicks have kickbacks.

What's Smart?

In no place is this more true than it is with sex. My letter file is loaded with proof of this hard fact. Here are three somber witnesses who learned the hard way that life doubles back.

The first is an unmarried father. Number two is a girl with a broken heart. The third is a mother who writes for all girls everywhere.

LETTER ONE

I got this girl pregnant, see, and I offered to marry her, but she said she didn't love me that much. Now I feel like I have a terrible burden that can never be unloaded no matter what I try. She has gone away to have her baby, and I can hardly stand to think what happened.

LETTER TWO

When the time came to go to the hospital I didn't want to give up my baby, but I knew I had to. It was the unhappiest feeling anybody ever had. I felt like something fell apart inside me, but that isn't the worst. The worst is how I will always know there is a little boy somewhere and he is my son and where did he go?

"Buy now! Pay later!" There aren't many of us who haven't been lured by that come-on. It sounds so easy. Then comes payday. And if payday is every day, well, that's about the worst.

It is wise also to remember another thing about kicks. Some of them have *delayed* kickbacks.

"Boo! Remember me?"

Sometimes the inner voices shout it loud. Sometimes they push over the tombstones silently and follow on padded feet. Suddenly they're alive again to hunt us down and haunt us.

That's how this mother found it.

LETTER THREE

Dear Dr. Shedd:

I am writing to answer the girls who ask, "Why is it smart to save yourself till marriage?" I thought they ought to hear from someone who knows the answer by experience. Let me ask you girls some questions.

What if you didn't wait and you married somebody else and you had this guilty feeling that keeps eating on you and you can't get rid of it?

What if you knew in your heart that you should have told him before you were married only you didn't and now you feel you are living a lie?

What if you confessed to the priest but you keep getting these dreadful feelings of shame sometimes when you and your husband are together?

What if you have friends whose men are running around and you keep asking yourself, "Wouldn't it be too bad if mine did that? I really deserve it, don't I? Will I be punished for what I did wrong?"

What if you had a daughter and she is beginning to date? What if you would like to talk to her about these things but you get tongue-tied because you feel like you don't have a right to say anything?

What if you keep wondering whether you will ever get this straightened out in your heart so things can be right between you and your daughter? Between you and your husband? Between you and God?

Do you see what I mean? The trouble with sex before marriage is that it can't be treated as casually as you think it can now. Sometimes it lives to hunt you down and haunt you. Then it grows and it seems like an octopus. It has many arms and they reach a long way and they grow tighter as the years pass. They seem to be crushing part of you which you think could be wonderful if only you could go back and live it over again.

The reason I know what could happen to you is that I have a husband who is beginning to get ideas and I can't help wondering if this is partly because I have never been able to let myself go with him. I also have a daughter I can't relate to and I know she feels bad about it like I do.

That is why I know it is smart to save yourself till marriage.

A Worried Mother

Three sad souls with an important message. And they need no further words from me. Only I thought it might be good to share the way one boy put it. We had been exchanging some thoughts on kickbacks and this is what he said:

■ IF I DIG WHAT YOU'RE SAYING, YOU MEAN SOME KICKS HAVE A VERY LONG LEG AND A REAL HARD FOOT!

4

It's Smart to Decide
What Your Limits Will Be

Here is an arrangement of four sentences I would like to stamp
on your mind—
You can let yourself go if you decide to!
You can choose who you let it go to!
You can do it as often as you want to!
But you only do it first one time!
Judging from my mail there are many to whom "Number One"
means something extra special.
Like this girl:

The awful part is what I am going to tell you now. Now I have
met another boy who I know is much more right for me than Johnny
ever was. Only I don't know what to do. He shares all his problems
with me, and I would like to share mine with him. But it would be
terrible if I told him about Johnny and me, and he decided I am not
so much of a person as he is looking for.

I guess what I am saying is that I feel like I left part of me with
Johnny, and I would give anything to have it back so I could share
my whole self with Steve. Do you know what I almost wish? I almost
wish he would tell me about him and some other girl. Then he would

understand how easy it is to make a mistake. I never did intend to go so far. Why didn't I look ahead and save myself?

"Why?" That question comes my way again and again. "Why? Why? Why?"

One reason why is the failure to "pre-think" sex. What I mean is you should have some solemn sex agreements with yourself. You can do this by asking right now, "What kind of person do I want to be for the man or woman I marry?" Then when you have decided that, you will know some other things. You will know whether to draw lines and where the "No Trespassing" signs have to go.

In the life of the average teenager there will be some intense moments. When they come, the only help available may be your predetermined policy. What you are may *show up* in the crisis. But it is almost sure to have been *made up* long before you got there.

So, let's consider some lines you can draw now which might help you later.

You may have heard "rules" from people you run around with that go something like this: "Messing around is O.K., but only with your clothes on" or "Anything above the waist is all right." Not bad, but are rules like these explicit enough? What most of the crowd means by "messing around" is "everything but." No matter how you title it, the object is sexual stimulation without intercourse. It starts with hands below the neck. From there it goes to hands on the naked body, then to the sex organs. In its final stages it is satisfied only with "climax."

For this reason every girl who begins to get serious needs to know something about a boy's hands. What she needs to know is that they are part of the male sexual equipment. Allowed free movement, they may call out more response than she wants to let go.

Naturally this doesn't happen all at once. It may take weeks, months, a year or more. But those who begin seriously "messing around" will find out. This stuff is devastatingly progressive. Tomorrow night you must go a little farther for the same thrills you got tonight. Next week you won't be satisfied with last week's excitement. Hundreds, and I do mean hundreds, in the teen world have discovered, "Everything but" too often leads to "Everything gone."

It is not my purpose to scare you. If you're a typical teenager, you're nervous enough already. But I can promise you this. You won't be nearly so nervous if you pre-think your sex limits now.

You better, because you know it's a fact that nobody else is going to do this for you. Unless your folks go with you on every date, unless they never let you out of their sight, unless they devise some other method to keep you under constant surveillance, what you do with sex is yours to decide.

That's why I say you are smart to predetermine right now how far you will go!

5

It's Smart to Be Sure
When You're Ready for Marriage

One of my favorite Sunday school happenings is the one about this little boy whose teacher reminded the class, "Now remember children, we are here to help others." To which the small sharpie replied, "What are the others here for?"

From his viewpoint this was a logical question. It is natural for a child to think first of himself. Sure, he may have periods of generosity, but these are only flashes. Most of the time he thinks in terms of "Me first. Me second. Me third." Which sounds awful, and it is.

Unfortunately, whether you like it or not, this reaches its peak during your teen years. Unless you are very unusual, one of your distinguishing marks right now is *selfishness!*

Another way to spell it is *trouble.* Anywhere you look, they go together. World problems, race riots, neighborhood fights, marital breakdown—wherever you find selfishness, you'll find trouble.

Now put your ear down close because here comes the punch line. *The trouble in teen sex is selfishness!*

For the average teenage boy, sex is a matter of "getting." "Did you *get* a little?" . . . "Are you *getting* any?" . . . "I'm going out

What's Smart?

and *get* me some!" . . . These are a common part of teen male talk.

Girls aren't much better. She may say, "I let him because I love him," or "I gave in because I care so much." But the chances are that, at this age, she is caring about herself caring about him.

If you could read my letters from teen girls; if you could listen to the ones I work with personally; you would see what I mean. Always the predominant words are "I," "Me," "Myself." That's how it goes. When the subject is possible marriage, whether it's girl or boy, the question usually reads, "Does he have what *I* need?" . . . "Do you think she would make *me* a good mate?"

What's the matter with that? The matter is that it is only half good enough. There is a second part which is every bit as important. Would you believe that I almost never hear it from anyone under twenty? This is the mature kind of question which asks, "Am I what *he* needs?" . . . "Do I have what's right for *her*?" . . . "At my present stage of development *am I quite fit yet for anyone?*"

Before we leave this, let me tell you my favorite from this file. For immature thinking this deserves a special prize. What she said was, "I want a one-hundred-percent guarantee that he will make me one-hundred-percent happy one hundred percent of the time." Which you will agree, deserves some kind of cup for one-hundred-percent silly!

Great marriage is not like that. It is, rather, the work of two imperfect craftsmen shaping their dream together. They hammer their conflicts into harmony. They mend their breaks with mercy. They laugh and they suffer and they argue and they work. They work and they work and they work and they work hard. And if it's mature love in mature marriage, it is working hardest at this— to overcome selfishness, to care honestly how the other person feels. Always, transferring "I" to "We" to "You" is the toughie, the real hard work.

Another letter I get often is the sincere inquiry about how to know for sure. Here is a winsome line typical of these letters. It is written by a teenage girl debating whether she should go ahead with marriage. He's pushing. She's wondering. In these few words she seems to sum up so much for so many:

Can you tell me how I can be absolutely sure I should get married? I mean, can you tell me so there wouldn't be any question whatsoever? If you could tell me that, I would be so grateful.

I wish I could, but I can't. Nobody can. The reason is that it finally comes back to the same old conclusion. Some things you have to decide for yourself.

Since that is true I'm going to ask *you* some questions. If you will get as quiet as you can inside; if you will try your best to be honest; you might be helped more by your answers than my answers. So here goes:

QUESTIONS FOR A TEENAGER THINKING ABOUT MARRIAGE

■ Do I think more about what I can get than what I can give? Is it possible for me to care sincerely about another person's happiness? Most of the time am I loving for what I get out of it? Am I willing to sacrifice some of my wants without feeling resentful? Do I tend to use other people for my own needs?

■ Do I want to let myself go? Am I ready to open the doors way down in my heart? Do I understand that the key to healthy marriage is full communication? How honest am I willing to be in sharing what's inside me?

■ Can I give words to my love freely? Is it easy for me to express appreciation? If it isn't, will I give it my best effort and keep trying? Am I tender enough to meet the needs of this person I might marry? Do I want to know what blocks the flow of my affection?

■ When there are differences between me and others, what do I do? Can I look inside myself to see where I might be wrong? Do I surface my hostilities by blaming others, or can I bring them out in a healthy manner? Have I learned the mature way to say, "I don't like that" . . . "I do not agree" . . . "Let's discuss it"?

■ Do I cherish liberty for other people? Am I overly possessive? Too domineering? Jealous to excess? If I'm like that, am I willing to trace the reasons inside me? Am I mature enough to let the other person grow individually while we grow together?

What's Smart?

■ My ideas of success, are they healthy? Am I ambitious enough? or overambitious? Do I drive too hard? or am I lazy? Is there any tendency to perfectionism in me and, if so, do I know why? Does money mean more than it should? Am I willing to adjust my goals to another person's goals so that we will both be better people?

■ Are my religious feelings my own or only something borrowed? Do they go deep enough or are they simply surface stuff? Have I worked out my philosophy of life with enough care? Is my concept of the universe big and growing? Do I feel a genuine sense of responsibility to Someone greater than myself? Are my attitudes here adjustable? Could they blend with another person's to the betterment of us both?

If you're overwhelmed, I'm rather glad, really. The kind of relationship you want is every bit as big as that barrage of questions.

To be awed at how great love is . . . this is one of the first requirements for mature marriage.

One final word on this subject. Always when I am with teens, this question comes through loud and clear: "How can I know when I'm really in love?" And though the question may be framed in varied versions, the real query is: "When does a relationship have enough solid ingredients for a good marriage?"

Since this is one of the prime questions, I wrote a book called *How to Know If You're Really in Love*. This book, reviewed in a recent *Reader's Digest* and featured on numerous television shows, presents ten tests. Each of these ten tests is printed in duplicate, so you and your friend can fill in answers individually and then compare notes. They are: *Transparency, Liberty, Unselfishness, Mercy, Apology, Sexuality, Money, Distance, Fun,* and *Holiness.*

If you are at the point where you are in love and asking, "How do I know if this is the real thing?", reading this book and taking the ten tests may help you decide.

II

The Dignity of Your
Own Judgment

II

The Dignity of Your Own Judgment

Introduction

One day Karen came home excited. They had been studying dinosaurs and there was this one character with a funny build. Up front he was all power—mammoth chest, muscular neck, big head. He had teeth that could crunch trees like celery. But along about his middle he began to run out of stuff. His hind quarters were weak. They were something of a drag. Still, that wasn't all of him. He had a long tail which seemed like it would never end. And the weird thing was that *his brain was in the tip of his tail.*

You can see at once that he would be some kind of problem. It took so long for his front to get the message. When he started to smash things up, the hold orders came too late.

I've forgotten the name of his species, and I'm not even sure I got it all straight. But this is the truth—he's a good illustration of the teenager and sex!

Biologically you're ready. Physically you're capable. Yet the question is, "Are your brains up front? Is there too much gap between what you can do and what you should do?"

We all know this is a fact with sex and many things. Some people know a lot but don't know how to handle what they know. They've got plenty of data but too little sense.

Good judgment is combining information and action in the right way at the right time. This is a big order for a teenager. But if you learn it during these years you stamp yourself as something special. At any age there is real dignity in developing your self-respect to the maximum. I hope some of the things we will look at now will help you to do that.

1

Basic Differences—Male and Female!

There is a favorite illustration about sex differences which is done with two lines. If you draw a horizontal black line, that's how it is with the boys. If you draw a colored line up and down from that one—now above, now below, now even with—that's how it goes for the girls.

In other words, the male is constant. Almost always you'll find him the same way about sex. That is, interested and ready to go. His feelings are right there below the surface.

With the female there is considerable variation. Her whole system operates out of a rhythm. If she's like most of her gender, her feelings will probably fluctuate. These ups and downs may be monthly. They might be even more variable. But this is all part of her nature.

Sometimes girls write me like this: "It seems all he ever thinks about is sex. Just for kicks the other night I tried this experiment. I brought up ten different subjects and timed him. I wanted to see how long it would take him to turn each one of them around to sex. He really is a great conversationalist. He's also very smart. In fact, I'm crazy about him. But the longest was seven minutes, and I'm beginning to wonder. Do you think he's dangerous?"

Sometimes boys write me like this: "We are both active in our churches, and we have decided to wait till we're married. I really do love her and I know she loves me. Only sometimes she hardly lets me touch her. Then sometimes I can hardly keep her off me. In fact, whenever she's like this I'm glad it's me she's with. I wouldn't want to hurt her but boy am I tempted. Tell me, are all girls like that and what should I do?"

Well, he's not a sex maniac and she's not a manic-depressive. (Way up! Way down!) They sound quite normal to me.

All of which is how it is and that's how it will always be. Which means what? Which means that a wise teenager accepts the inevitable, quits trying to change what can't be changed, and thanks God for the mystery.

That's about it, I think, except for one thing more. My teenagers say I should tell it to you like I told it to them. It goes like this: A boy can start with sex and it might end there. But if he really cares about the girl, he may want more than sex. Then his feelings move to love. With the girl it is usually the opposite. She starts with love and her sex thoughts are brought in later. In other words, her feelings begin in her heart, move to her head where it's easier for her to think it over, and then it may become sex. His feelings often start with sex; then if he can calm himself enough, he'll think it over too, and then finally he may feel what she feels.

Here is a good agreement for a serious couple after they are married: *He'll teach her how to love with her body! She'll teach him how to love with his soul!*

2

You Can't Tell How It Will Be

Here are two paragraphs from letdown teenagers. The first is from a boy. Number two comes from a girl.

I want to ask you, what is so great about sex? I heard all this talk, so I decided to find out. I knew where I could get some so I did. Only when it was over all I could think of was, "Phooey! That wasn't so hot." Why all the excitement?

He said it would be like heaven and I would get the biggest thrill. So we did, and I guess he felt something. But the fact is, I didn't feel anything, only bewildered.

Tough luck for them, wasn't it? But the line forms over here and it's a long line.

I am not trying to tell you that teen sex is a total collapse. For some this is not true. But for every one of the winners there are literally hundreds who echo—"Phooey! That wasn't so hot!" . . . "I didn't feel anything, only bewildered."

And the problem is that you can't tell ahead of time how it will be. But if you could read my letters you would come to this conclusion: it isn't worth the gamble!

THE STORK IS DEAD

This is especially true on the girl's side. His chances of satisfaction are a great deal better than hers. So, if you're a girl and you're debating, tune in right here:

Don't listen to this guy who is promising so much. The chances are good he can't deliver. Unless he's a very experienced hand, you're in for big disappointment. And even if he knows what he's doing, he doesn't know how you'll do. Nobody knows, including you! *There is only one path to the kind of sex you want. This is the path to the altar and a permanent relationship. Sex at its best is a long-term thing. It calls for total commitment.*

Often I hear from adults who are working with young people. This is always a special kind of thrill. Many of these are experts whose advice is worth hearing. This one is.

Dear Dr. Shedd:

Some girls brought me your column from *Teen* magazine and asked me to lead a discussion on "free love" at their next club meeting. This is not unusual since I am a doctor who works with teenagers.

I have read what you say with interest and I thought you might like to know one thing I am including in the notes for my talk.

A girl needs to be told that this boy who is using every means at his disposal to talk her into sex doesn't have the slightest idea how it is going to be with her. He feels a powerful urge and he is sure it will be a great experience for him. Chances are that he is right about that. But if my experience as a doctor means anything, the odds are somewhere near one hundred percent that she won't get anything but scared, or emotionally scarred from shame and remorse, or pregnant. The reason is that biologically girls are put together in such a way that sex needs the protection of marriage, a home, a deep and trusting relationship to make it right for them.

If you feel that this thought has merit, I would appreciate your passing it on to your readers.

Dr. J. B., Pennsylvania

3

Lines Guys Use (For Girls Only. Particularly Younger Teens)

If you could put your ear down to the letters on my desk you'd be amazed. One of the things you'd hear are sweet words like you wouldn't believe. The lines guys use are really something.

To satisfy my curiosity I did some research. Could these smooth sayings be put in any kind of order?

They could and that's what I'm about to tell you. I must admit that I feel like a traitor. After all, way back there, I was a boy too. But I asked a few in our church group and they gave me the green light. One of them even said, "I could use a few suggestions."

So here's how they go. They are the lines guys use to get this young thing to go further.

■ THE WOUNDED PIGEON. His line is *The world is so unfair. See how they pick on me. Nobody treats me right but you.* It takes very little of this to appeal to your mothering instinct . . . You feel like you did that day you found the baby robin fallen from its nest . . . life has been tough for him . . . parents so cruel . . . nobody understands. One common variation is the boy your folks object to—he has a bad reputation. Maybe he's been in trouble with the law. But it really wasn't his fault—"They" did it. Or he may even swing it around to "Please reform me"! . . . "Make me your project"! . . . "I'll probably die if you leave me." But whatever the version, you watch out! When he plays to your sympathy like crazy; when you know he'd really be fractured if you did call it off; when you're smothering him with comfort, you may be ready for the pushover. This line appears over and over in my letters—"But I felt *so* sorry for him!"

■ THE "POOR LITTLE YOU" LINE. The opposite of the wounded pigeon . . . *You have never been loved right . . . Your folks, brothers, sisters, teachers, grandmother, stepmother, the whole world—they've given you such a bad deal. I'm so sorry. Poor little unloved you.*

Common variation: *Too bad your folks don't get along, dear. But there is such a thing as true love and I can prove it to you right here in this car! . . .*

Especially dangerous (a) if you come from an unhappy home; (b) if you dislike your mother; (c) if you have never been as close to your father as you would like to be; (d) if he catches you when you're feeling sorry for yourself.

Anytime you hear, "I'll help you through these troubled waters" coming from a male, you be careful. And when you begin to think, "But he understands me *so* perfectly" rising out of your own heart, this is the time for a retake. We're glad he understands, and you don't want one who doesn't. But be sure he understands a lot more— like right and wrong and the sacredness of life.

■ THE "CAMPUS SNOW MAN" LINE. *How lucky can you be? So many girls are dying to go out with me.* He probably wouldn't say it out loud but you get the message. He's handsome, personable, great smile, class officer, student council, team captain, top athlete, divine dancer, may be an excellent scholar . . . he makes you feel like somebody special. It's all so exciting when the gang says, "Look who she's going out with!"

This could be a fine boy who doesn't know he's snowing you . . . or maybe he isn't fine. Some of these special jobs use their God-given talents in the wrong way.

Particularly dangerous for girls (a) very young, (b) inexperienced, (c) inferiority complex.

The Dignity of Your Own Judgment

■ THE "ALL FOR YOUR COUNTRY" LINE. *I'm waiting my call to the battlefront. This is my contribution. What would you like to contribute?* He probably drops this kind of thing casually. It is more effective if he suffers in silence—you can feel how he hurts. So brave. So uncomplaining . . . Look what he's giving up! How could you refuse to give up one little thing when his very life is threatened?

Warning: Be especially leery of these flag-wavers when they're in uniform or on the last dates before they leave.

■ THE "PROVE YOUR LOVE OR I GO AWAY" LINE. This could be as old as Adam . . . you can bet the boys were using it back in the days of the prehistoric monsters. There must be at least a million witnesses, living and dead, who would say: (1) If he does get what he wants, he may leave you anyway; (2) If he gets what he wants and doesn't leave you, you still don't have much. Be careful! This guy is murder. He's a slow, steady operator and you're almost over the hill when you begin to feel, "It would *just kill me* if I lost him!"

■ THE "EVERYBODY DOES IT" LINE. *What's the matter with you anyway? You come over with the Puritans or something? Join the party! Live a little!* These are the "new morality" boys, the "situational ethics" crowd, the "liberated." They get you worried that the glad stuff is on and you're missing it . . . they poke fun at your training, chop away at your roots, offer you a ticket to the "in" crowd.

Variation: *You don't want to just sit home all the time, do you? If you're looking for dates, you gotta go get with it!*

■ THE "LET ME MAKE A WOMAN OUT OF YOU" LINE. Variations: *I am about to complete your life, darling . . . Let me be your teacher . . . You are so great but there is this one thing lacking.*

This character may be an ace at combining all the sophistication pitches . . . "Look no farther! You have found me! I'm just the one to induct you into the mysteries of womanhood!" He leaves you with the feeling that if you only had what he offers then you'd have it all!

■ THE "MEN WANT EXPERIENCED WOMEN" LINE. *All the fellows these days prefer girls who know how to do it.* These come in several varieties: (1) Sinister types who know what they're up to; (2) Pure phonies who don't know what they're up to; (3) "Little or no regard for women" boys; (4) Plain dumb; (5) Guys who think you're plain dumb.

The truth? This gambit is built on a totally false premise. The good ones usually don't want experienced women. If you hear this pitch, back off and take a long look. When this character settles down and decides to marry, he usually looks for somebody moral!

■ THE "WE'RE GOING TO GET MARRIED ANYWAY" APPROACH. *What's a little slip of paper between people like us? We'll make it legal some time anyway.* Label this an "approach" rather than "line" because it is so gradual you're involved before you know what happened . . . most of the time this is that really nice guy you're *sure* is the right one . . . very common in the long-time steady relationships.

Questions: What if you *might* meet someone you like better? . . . Or what if he did? Good return from your side: "But, Jimmy, I love you so much I wouldn't want you ever to feel obligated to me."

■ THE "YOU ARE OBVIOUSLY FRIGID" LINE. Every all-everything girl hopes to be all woman some day. So he gets you worried. Horrors! Wouldn't it be too bad if you actually *are* undersexed? . . . "Panic button, where are you?" . . . "What if I am left on the shelf! That would be simply awful."

Warning: The guy who can get you feeling like this may be a real "pro" whose concept of womanhood is that "girls are things to be used." If you marry one of these, chances are good he'll *make* you frigid. Plenty of married women could tell you it's true. There is nothing to produce cold chills like this guy. He only loves himself while he pretends to be loving you.

■ THE "SEX DISCUSSER." He gets you talking about sex, thinking sex, verbalizing sex . . . excellent conversationalist . . . promotes heavy "think" sessions . . . philosopher . . . stirs you with synonyms and wows you with metaphors.

"Whoa, back!" . . . you may get so excited you can hardly wait . . . words may lead you to the point where you act out your discussion as a natural sequence. Some of these are smoothies who do it deliberately; others are innocents who don't know what's happening; but when it begins to feel too "natural," this could be the time for a screeching halt.

■ THE "ANYTHING WE DO IS O.K. SO LONG AS WE DON'T GO ALL THE WAY" LINE. Great pair of hands . . . varies from wide experience to none at all, but he's got an amazing skill at turning you on . . . gives you thrills you've never known before . . . expert in the erogenous zones . . . fabulous sensations. *You can never get pregnant this way so how could it be wrong?* How it could be wrong is (a) some feelings are for marriage alone; (b) you might get so stirred you lose your head *and* your virginity; (c) premarital intercourse isn't the only sin; (d) some habits developed now will hamper you later.

We could go on and on but you get the idea. Lines guys use come in numberless styles with countless variations.

The "flatterer" turns your pretty head with this line: "There are millions of women in the world. But they are so ordinary. You alone have what it takes to send me."

The "gland boys" pitch their case on the old saw that it's unhealthy to repress your feelings (mostly his).

The "so silent, so mysterious, so self-contained" character drives you out of your mind to know him better.

So they run the gamut from those who know what they're about, to those who stumble onto your weakness, to those like you who are totally innocent. Incidentally, that "two babes in the woods" thing may be a deadly combination. These "special secrets, just us two" can be treacherous.

Boys! They really are all the great things you call them. But you better believe it, they are a lot of other things too. They are put together with powerful drives. And as though that were not enough, their keen male senses are forever at it. They go on searching, zigging, zagging. This is only one more thing that makes them fascinating. But don't get so enthralled you turn your brain off. You keep thinking, you hear?

Question: Are there any new lines?

Since the first edition of *The Stork Is Dead,* I've picked up some with new slants. This is from a recent letter (touches of "how lucky can you be"):

Dear Dr. Shedd:

You asked us to tell you if we heard any new lines. Well, I did. I was going with this character who kept telling me, "If you'd only say 'yes,' I promise nobody could ever turn you on the way I could turn you on. Wouldn't it be too bad if you missed the greatest?"

You may think that is so dumb nobody would go for it, but I will tell you what happened. He kept saying it in so many different ways, I almost hate to admit this, but it finally began to get to me. Sometimes I caught myself asking, what if I *am* missing the greatest? That's when I decided I better cross him off my list with a big red pencil. So I did.

(Important reverse: Girls can be over-pushy too. Fact: Generally the male is the more aggressive, but not always. Sometimes in subtle ways and some not so subtle, the female "come-on" may need some strong man-handling.)

4

Why Girls Give In

Did you notice how many of the lines guys use are aimed at a particular target? At the center of a woman's heart is her longing to matter to some male. That's how they're made, and it's the greatest thing ever for men. But it isn't so great for girls unless they handle it right.

There are several places where this might be worth checking. Most of my "Why did I do it?" letters fall into one of these categories.

■ THE "IT HONESTLY DOES MEAN EVERYTHING" REASON. Here is a nice, nice girl in love with a fine, fine boy. They have a good thing going and they both know it. He needs her and she needs him. They are first-rate people, loving each other sincerely.

This is the reason why most girls give in. Sure, they want to hold the line and they try. Sometimes their love "plateaus" for a while, and during these times they can manage. Then suddenly they are catapulted into an even greater oneness. It is good, satisfying, meaningful.

So what can be done about it?

If you've gone too far and there seems no way back, maybe you need help. I hope you find it. Particularly, I hope you can go home together and talk it out with your parents. You know that won't work? Are you sure? Have you approached all four parents? Have you said, "We're face to face with a problem. We think you should know. Can't we talk it over? We need your help."

But obviously the time to avoid a crisis in young love is long before it arrives. As we have said before, smart couples pace their relationship. Two educations, maybe one service stint, or just growing up—these all take time. Sometimes I am sorry that life does us like it does. But certain facts don't change because we wish them another way.

There is, however, one piece of good news I have for you. This is a rule of life which will not fail you if you don't fail it.

Rule: *Your longing controlled till things are right can result in thrilling things for your marriage!*

■ THE "DAUGHTER LONESOME FOR FATHER" REASON. If you could have seen Sally operate you would have known she was overdoing. The way she walked, the way she talked, the way she dressed—it was a bit much! But it wasn't all sex like it looked on the surface. In fact, she herself put it this way: "I think the trouble was that I had a crush on my father only he didn't notice. He was hardly ever home and he was wild about golf. He had this huge business and he did a lot *for* me. But he never did anything *with* me. Could this be why I've been such a flirt?"

She was sitting there in my study when she said it. She had come for help. The night before she had a terribly close call. So she talked and I thrilled . . . "I'm strong here, weak there. I can handle this, I should watch that." This kind of honesty is very rare for a teenager. But to know where you're vulnerable can be one of your greatest assets.

Maybe your parents had nothing to do with your particular problem. It might have been one of a thousand other things. But do turn around sometimes and evaluate your background. Something made you the way you are today. Do you know what? If you're a girl and you turn on fast, this is a rule worth considering:

The Dignity of Your Own Judgment

Rule: *When you are boy-crazy, what you may need more than boys is to know what made you lonesome!*

■ THE "GENERAL INFERIORITY" REASON. Here is something we could say of the whole human race. Everybody in the world feels below average sometimes. We don't have to wonder what these girls mean:

> I would give *anything* if I could be one of the 'in' crowd.

(Don't you wish she didn't mean "anything"? I regret to report she did.)

> See how awful I look? I know I must have six million freckles.

(She sent me her picture and I thought she was cute. I happen to like freckles, and so do lots of guys I know.)

> I have had this awful loneliness inside me ever since I can remember.

(This is one of the worst things a girl can say unless she understands what she's saying.)

All of which says that evaluating ego needs is important all the time. It is especially true if some boy is beginning to read you. Some of them are experts at this. They may do it instinctively. Others learn it as an art. But what you better do is beat them to it. Don't quit until you know the answer to these all-important questions: "My need for affection: is it normal?" "My longing to be liked: is it healthly?" "My desire for attention: am I pushing too hard?"

If you think you are overloaded here, you be wise and take it to someone. Perhaps your school counselor, doctor, minister, or an older friend could give you an assist. Maybe they could even show you some strong points you've been overlooking. Under that avalanche of "poor, poor me" there might be a buried treasure. Sharing your problem is no sign of weakness. It's really a very smart move.

But whether you get help or figure it out yourself, there is one inescapable conclusion. Inferiority feelings and sex activity are often seen together. Many a person discovered that truth too late. Others, like Sally, saw it in the nick of time. If you haven't noticed it yet, then sit down right now and consider.

Rule: *The girl who uses sex to bolster her ego, won't!*

5

Ways to Say "No!"

It makes me shudder a little when I hear from girls who say, "He thinks too much of me to do anything wrong."

May his tribe increase. But don't count on it. I know any number of pregnant girls who could witness that sometimes noble resolves *do* cave in. From what I see of teenage love, you can count on this—generally, the girl must keep her cool or the boy won't be able to.

The stork is dead means a lot of things. One thing it means is that boys are boys everywhere. So it's safest to figure that "How far would she go?" is a standard question with most males.

This does not mean that boys are basically bad. If you have picked up that idea somewhere, turn it off. The truth is more in this direction—most boys you'll be dating won't be bad unless you let them. Or, let's say they'll be as good as you make them be.

So, how does a girl hold the line?

I asked a group of "In" teenagers how they do it. There were some great answers. Things like, "When he starts the French kissing, I chew bubble gum" . . . "I try to switch his attention! Get him interested in something else. Suggest some keen place to go, something great to do!" . . . "I just begin to cry. That usually works for me!"

But the ones whose answers have the feel of the real said this is no place to be indefinite. They put it like this: "Most boys understand what 'No' means" . . . "Giving it to him straight is the only way!" . . . "I try to deliver the message real sweet, but firm!" . . . "I agree with him that sex is great, but I make it plain that this part of me just isn't for him, at least not till we're married" . . . "I find that it works sometimes to get into a discussion of sex and all that sort of thing. If I can get him talking, it's funny how the serious side cools it" . . . "If he doesn't respect my 'No,' I figure I haven't lost much if I lose him." Then there was this cutie from a real sophisticate, "The line I use is, 'Harry, you're really getting to me! But I've heard it won't work unless you do it with energy and right now I don't have the energy!' "

All of which says again—keep your head screwed on and your brains turning over. Teenage sex is no light matter.

As I think back over the accounts I've heard of clever young ladies and their pushy young lovers, there is one story I simply must tell you. This is a true tale of a girl who thought up a most ingenious turnoff.

When he was about to take it by force, she pulled this slicker. "O.K. But first I have to go to the all-night drug store. I know what to use only I don't have any. I'm really protecting *you,* see? You don't want to get me pregnant. I'm sure we'll both enjoy it more if we don't have that worry, etc. etc."

So the poor sap fell for all this and here's how I know: *when she got to the drugstore she phoned me to come to her rescue!*

One night in a meeting of girls, I told her story. Several years later I received this interesting letter from one of that group. She was in college now and this is how she did it:

Dr. Shedd, Do you remember that story you told us about the girl and her all-night drug store? Well you will never know how glad I am you told it. The same thing happened to me with this boy I'm dating. He's a Phys. Ed. major and so strong.

What happened was he got carried away the other night and I couldn't stop him. So I remembered what you told us. Only there aren't any all-night drug stores so I said the filling station. But when we got there I didn't want to embarrass him. So I got out of the car and stood by his door and told him I would call the police. Do you know what happened? It scared him so bad he started to cry. Really I felt so sorry for him. But by now he forgot all about sex and he took me home like a lamb. I thought I should write you this just in case you want to tell some others. Thanks again.

The only word I could add is this one you see around sometimes—THIMK!

One more thing. Parents, especially mothers, ask, "But doesn't the boy have some responsibility too?" To which there is only one answer. He certainly does! Yet this is one certain truth: Too often he will not take any more responsibility than she takes. So I stand by this statement: *She,* who is very wise, increases *her* resistance as his pressure increases.

6

Why Won't They Let Us Go Steady?

"Why won't they let us go steady?" It seems like such an innocent little question, doesn't it? Yet it's no news to you that this can lead to one awful conflict.

So what does going steady have to do with sex?

Do I hear some teen replying, "Nothing! That's what makes me mad. Why can't my folks trust me? They got dirty minds, or something?"

Maybe they just know more than you know. Like, maybe they know what happens when two people get closer and closer. Maybe they've felt the power of closeness like you wouldn't know yet, and shouldn't.

What you have felt is the first soft touch and you like it. So you go back for more and this is even nicer. Then you feel it growing stronger, and this is better yet and more is even better. This is the object of going steady. Increasing warmth; greater security; a closer closeness.

Yet, you also know this when you think it through: Closeness is not confined to the mind. It has to be more than heads together, eyes looking, hands holding. If it's the kind of love worth caring about, it is constantly on the increase.

Parents know this. That's why they're anxious. In order not to care they would have to be: (a) secretly wishing you out of their hair; (b) not concerned enough (some kids tell me this really is hell); (c) plain stupid!

Sure, I know there are different kinds of going steady. If I get the reading right, one kind calls for exclusive dating. Then there is "going steadily," which is somewhat less of a tiedown. Each is free to date others under an agreement between them.

But I know this for certain and so do you. Some very sorry teenagers have used nice-sounding labels to cover up the facts. Which is strictly no good. The stork is dead! Sex and going steady do need to be thought through together.

It is a fact that certain kinds of people are strictly low voltage. Put them together anywhere; explain the rules; tell them they're on their own; give them a pat on their steady little heads and worry no more. There *are* combinations like that. If yours is one of these then I say, "Sure! Go steady!"

But if you're in the host where this doesn't apply; or if you were, but you're moving the other way; then come along and let's look a bit deeper. We'll call this:

▮ DANGER SIGNALS WHEN YOU'RE GOING STEADY

1. Your relationship is moving in the wrong direction if you are: *Cutting yourself off from many wonderful friendships because of this one friendship.* As soon as you begin to narrow your attention to one teenager, be careful. When more and more of your time is focused on a single person, be careful. If you are crowding out others, brushing old friends aside, be careful. This could be the signal that you have quit growing. It is important for you at your age to learn all kinds of people. Are you reducing your present contacts to your own future detriment?

2. Your relationship is moving in the wrong direction if you are: *reaching the point with each other where nothing else matters but being together.* This may sound like we're saying the first point over. But it's a bigger thing here than people. Teen years are for expanding,

trying on ideas, developing new interests, testing, proving. Sure you've got a great thing going. But is this great thing limiting your interest in other great things? Test questions: Is going steady giving me one thing I like but taking away others I need? Am I so swept up in this one experience that I am becoming lopsided?

3. Your relationship is moving in the wrong direction if you are: *increasingly stimulated sexually at too fast a speed for the time you have before you.* So, what does that mean? What that means is that together you better face up to this question, "How far away is our marriage?" You'll know what I mean when I say that cadence is all-important. That wonderful increasing crescendo is a beautiful part of true love. But it better be paced with firm orders. And you know it's a fact: Sometimes the only orders that count are your own orders to you!

7

What Is It Like
To Be Married at Seventeen?

Many letters come across my desk with variations on the theme: "What do you think of teen marriages?"

Like a lot of other things—I think they are great when they are great.

I have known some fine ones. I can think of a happy couple on a midwest farm. She was fifteen and pregnant. He was sixteen and scared silly. But she refused to give up her baby so he agreed to "do right."

Of course both sets of parents were humiliated. Still they said they would help make the best of it. So they went through with it. That was fifteen years ago. Today they have three children; a farm they are buying; some very happy memories; and "a thousand battle scars from trying to grow up too soon together." (That's the way she described it in their last anniversary letter.) But they *are* happy and I am proud of the job they've done.

I can think of another couple. He works in a radio factory. What he does is to solder wires all day long. What he wanted to do was to be an engineer. That was eleven years ago. He says it gets pretty dull and he wishes he could earn more money. She wants a better house. It would be nice, she thinks, if they could raise their children in a different neighborhood. He's crazy about cars, and man, would he like a new one. But she had an operation last year and they're still paying on that.

This is a fine couple. She is so attractive. He is so smart. If only he could get more schooling, he'd be a cinch for promotion. Someday, somehow, I hope things will be better for them, because I think they deserve it. It must be terribly grim seeing your dreams fade further and further into the future.

So there are two answers to "What do I think of teen marriages?" I could describe some others. But the trouble is when I finished with the next two, that would be it. Which is less than a handful, isn't it?

Honest, I'm not kidding! I have married a whole bunch of teens. What minister hasn't? And from the teens I've married; from the teens who write me; from the teens who have brought me their problems personally; I think your chances of a happy marriage at this age are practically nil.

Why don't teen marriages work out better? What makes them so generally unsuccessful? Well, there are lots of reasons and nobody knows them all.

But I know two and so do you. ONE IS A SAD GIRL WHO GAVE IN TOO SOON. ANOTHER IS AN IRRESPONSIBLE BOY WHO DIDN'T PROTECT HER.

In other words, gang, the *stork is dead!* Babies come from intercourse! Most teenagers get married because a baby is on the way. Most teenagers are not mature enough to be parents. How could they be? They weren't mature enough to perform responsibly. So here is another truth that seldom ever varies. Those who have to get married aren't old enough. *All of which is one more reason why I do not believe in sexual intercourse before marriage.*

But, you say, "This is an adult thinking! Grim, gruesome adult thinking!"

Then, since you must discount what I say because of my age, will you listen now to one of your own? We'll call her "X." I wish I could call her something else but I don't know her name. Her letter was anonymous. Still it is so good that after it appeared in *Teen* magazine, I had a phone call. It came from a well-known

The Dignity of Your Own Judgment

editor. She was impressed with the way this girl put words together. Would I please furnish name and address so she could contact her personally? She knew of a scholarship in a big university just waiting for someone like this.

So I hope she reads this because the editor is right. I know schools that would be glad to have her—magazines who need this kind of people on their staff—publishers who would be interested. In fact, all over the writing community, there are sources of help for people like this. So, "Come out! Come out! Wherever you are!" There are better things waiting for you.

Here's the letter now. I nominate this for one of the best letters I ever received. At least it has to be number one for poignancy. It seems to sweep up into one plaintive cry so many of the things we've been saying. This is the wisdom of one who is learning the hard way how much is involved in too-early sex.

Jimmy and I couldn't wait so now we are married. Big deal!

Let me tell you what it is like to be married at 17. It is like living in this dump on the third floor up and your only window looks out on somebody else's third floor dump.

It is like coming home at night so tired you feel like you're dead from standing all day at your checker's job. But you don't dare sit down because you might never get up again and there are so many things to do like cooking and washing and dusting and ironing. So you go through the motions and you hate your job and you ask yourself, "Why don't I quit?" and you already know why. It's because there are grocery bills and drug bills and rent bills and doctor bills, and Jimmy's crummy little check from the lumberyard won't cover them, that's why!

Then you try to play with the baby until Jimmy comes home. Only sometimes you don't feel like playing with her. But even if you do, you get this awful feeling that you are only doing it because you feel guilty. She is so beautiful, and you know it isn't fair to her to be in that old lady's nursery all day long. Then you wash diapers and mix formula and you hate it, and you wonder how long it will be till she can tell how you feel, and wouldn't it be awful if she could tell already?

Then Jimmy doesn't come home, and you know it's because he is out with the boys doing the things he didn't get to do because you had to get married. So, finally you go to bed and cry yourself to sleep telling yourself that it really is better when he doesn't come because sometimes he says the cruelest things. Then you ask yourself "Why does he hate me so?" And you know it is because he feels trapped, and he doesn't love you anymore, like he said he would.

Then he comes home and he wakes you up, and he starts saying all the nice things he said before you got married. But you know it is only because he wants something, and yet you want to believe that maybe it is the old Jimmy again. So you give in, only when he gets what he wants, he turns away and you know he was only using you once more. So you try to sleep but you can't. This time, you cry silently because you don't want to admit that you care.

You lie there and think. You think about your parents and your brothers and the way they teased you. You think about your backyard and the swing and the tree house and all the things you had when you were little. You think about the good meals your mother cooked and how she tried to talk to you, but you were so sure she had forgotten what it was like to be in love.

Then you think about your girl friends and the fun they must be having at the prom. You think about the college you planned to go to, and you wonder who will get the scholarship they promised you. You wonder who you would have dated in college and who you might have married and what kind of a job would he have?

Suddenly you want to talk, so you reach over and touch Jimmy. But he is far away and he pushes you aside, so now you can cry yourself to sleep for real.

If you ever meet any girls like me who think they are just too smart to listen to anyone, I hope you'll tell them that this is what it is like to be married at 17!

8

The Unusual

Dear Dr. Shedd:

This probably will be the awfullest letter you ever got, but I hope you won't mind because I need to know something.

This boy I am going with is great in some ways. We have talked a lot about sex, and I should tell you I have never done it and I won't until I am married and he knows that I mean it.

What is bothering me is that he wants to try some things. I hate to tell you what because it sounds so weird and I don't know how you would take it. What he says is that you can get the same feelings without doing it the regular way. I sure hope you know what I mean.

It goes on like that for several pages. Around and around the problem she goes but she never comes near the door. This happens often in my correspondence. "I sure hope you know what I mean" is a favorite teen expression. But you better drop it when the subject is sex. This is the place for straight talk.

So, let's have some.

Maybe what she means is *mutual masturbation*. This is the name for providing each other a climax without intercourse. It is done by manipulating each other's sex organs. More of this goes on than adults would like to admit.

There are several things wrong with it. One of the worst is that mutual masturbation often causes fixation. Physically and mentally we can get set in our ways. We are like the poor guy who refused to taste fried chicken. He wouldn't touch ice cream. He turned down all kinds of delightful foods. The reason was that he had been brought up on kidney beans. He liked them. In fact, he was crazy about them. So all his life all he ate was kidney beans. He missed all the other good things because he was hung up on beans.

I wouldn't try to persuade you that there is no physical gratification in mutual masturbation. That would not be true. What I am saying is that the half-pleasure you receive isn't worth it. Sex at its best is too fine a thing to jeopardize tomorrow for today.

This is the right place to say it again: it's your sex and what you do with it as a teenager is your decision. But I hope you will believe me right here. I know a lot of bean eaters who are "fixated" on beans. They cannot enjoy today's sex because of yesterday's substitutes. If you will reserve your sexual intimacies for marriage, you will be glad you did.

Another thing this boy could mean is *oral intercourse*. This is less common with young people than mutual masturbation. Yet it occurs frequently enough that you ought to know about it. What it means is that the mouth is used to provide pleasure and produce an orgasm. Kissing, licking, blowing, sucking can be another replacement for intercourse.

This is a natural part of sex play in many marriages. But you can believe it does more harm than good in pre-marital relationships. Generally the same objections apply which we covered in mutual masturbation, only more so.

In all of these unusual approaches, here is a rule you can depend on: The more intense a relationship is; the more it fascinates you with its peculiar aspects; the more likely you are to get stalled right there if you become involved before marriage.

It is important also for you to know about homosexuals and lesbians. A homosexual male is one who seeks physical gratification from another male. A homosexual woman, or lesbian, is a woman who wants sex with another woman. The term "homosexual" may be used for either men or women, but many prefer the term "gay," which can also apply to either men or women.

Some people have passed through a phase in their lives when they were bisexual, meaning sex either way. (The term "heterosexual" is properly used for those whose sexual activity is limited to the opposite sex.)

I often meet young people who are worried because they have had sexual experience with their own sex. Or they have experienced flashes of preference for someone of their own sex. Such occasional happenings do not make anyone a homosexual. However, if you are concerned at all about yourself, then you are wise to seek professional help. You are fortunate if your minister is a friend of young people. If that contact is not right for you, talk it over with a doctor or counselor who can guide you.

Experts disagree on why people are homosexual. Were they born this way? Some say yes. Others insist these preferences were shaped early in childhood, as early as two years of age. The fact is that, as of now, no one seems to have absolute answers. In many libraries, you can find books on almost any sexual pattern or preference. If you need to know more about these things, do study to learn all you can.

Some homosexuals and lesbians have become heterosexual. This usually requires professional help, although others witness to a change through a dynamic religious experience. The majority, however, say they are happy as they are and prefer to stay that way.

Contrary to what many people think, homosexuals and lesbians cannot always be recognized by effeminate or masculine behavior. Neither is someone with such mannerisms necessarily a homosexual. Since this is true, you will want to be especially careful to avoid labeling, gossip, and insensitive name-calling.

Someday a homosexual or lesbian may approach you for sex. If this happens, you would be wise to answer with a firm "no, thank you; this isn't for me." Then go your own way and turn them over to God. Derision or abuse is not the answer, either for them or for you.

Before we leave the unusual, we should say one thing more. This is for girls who might be *sexually approached by an older man*.

I am sorry to report that I hear these things too often. These letters are usually written when the surprised girl is still in shock. You can see at once that they are panicky. Like this:

> I am just floored. I have been baby-sitting for this family over a year and I can hardly believe it. Tonight when he was bringing me home he stopped the car and tried to make love. At first I thought I must be dreaming, but when I realized it was really happening, I almost died. He was always so nice before. Do you think it was because he had been drinking? What will I ever say when I see him again? Should I tell somebody? My daddy would probably kill him, and his wife is so nice. I don't know what to think. Can you tell me what to do?

This is just one of several versions of the same problem. A neighbor she always liked suddenly became over-amorous. Or a close friend of the family said something, did something very suggestive. Somebody she would never have suspected made passes which completely floored her.

What to do? Generally, when this happens, it is a good idea to do nothing until you have calmed down. Perhaps you will feel that you must talk with someone. Maybe you can't get it out of your system any other way. So, be discreet in selecting your counselor, and go ahead. They might help you decide whether it should be reported. Maybe it shouldn't.

But whatever else you do, I would try to be sympathetic. One mark of maturity is the ability to understand why people do wrong. Possibly your counselor will help you see this. Some married men are unhappy. Some overdrink. Some act on impulse and are sorry later. Some aren't as dangerous as they are foolish. Some should be reported because they are not safe. It's up to you, and your counselor if you have one, to make the decision. And the chances are that your best judgment will be as near right as you can get.

There is another "way-out" sex problem. Any man would be ashamed to admit that there are men like this around. But I decided that I should tell you because it shows up too often.

The Dignity of Your Own Judgment

This is *incest.* It means sex relations between members of the same family. The kind I hear about is usually between a stepfather and his stepdaughter. (Mother-son incest is not as frequent.) Most often the relationship is one of long standing. It probably started before the innocent child knew much about sex. Now grown to teen age, she wants out. What can she do?

The tough facts are that all the solutions are unpleasant ones. They are almost too much for a teenager. But the choices seem to be: (1) To run away; (2) To give up and let it go on; (3) To tell someone in the family (there is the chance that this might break up the home); (4) To seek legal help (incest is a criminal offense); (5) To stand up and say: "I am through. I've had it. It's over. You are guilty of a serious crime. If you leave me alone from now on, I do not intend to cause trouble. But if you touch me once more, I will throw the book at you. And remember, I've already taken enough from you. The time has come for me to meet boys and live normally. That's final."

Obviously, this kind of maturity is an awesome order for a teenager. But I have known several wonderful girls who did it. And without exception, when they made the decision to take their stand, a wonderful thing happened. They were given strength for that ordeal, plus a lot more.

These are sordid things to consider. But whatever you do, don't let the seamy side discourage you. Sure the bad is bad, but that's how it is. With some things, the worse a thing is at its worst, the finer it can be at its finest. That's how it is with sex.

9

Masturbation—Gift of God

Let's start with a definition: "Masturbation—Self-production of an orgasm by exciting the genital organs."

The reason for beginning here is that some young people actually do not know what it means. Usually these are among the younger teens. Sometimes they are late bloomers, those who develop slowly. So, let's state it clearly. Masturbation is sex by yourself.

Probably no phase of sex is more fuzzy in more minds. Here are some examples of the mis-truths, half-truths, and confusion. Most of these letters are from young teens. But one writer is a college sophomore.

My big brother says you will go crazy if you do it too many times. How many? . . . I can't even read a magazine without thinking about this. Do you think I might be some kind of sex fiend? . . . I heard if you do it too often you might as well not get married because you couldn't do it right. Please tell me if that is so . . . My mother found this magazine in my room and she raised so much cain I was mortified. Then she showed it to my father. He said if they ever caught me again he would beat me terrible. I am so scared . . . I have tried to stop and even promised God I would. But it seems like the harder I try the worse it gets . . . My friend said everyone can tell when you do it by the way you hold your mouth. Is that true?

This could go on a long time. So let's get it out from behind the haze for an open look. There are several things you should know:

■ *Masturbation is practically universal.*

No matter how we define it, this is a very common practice. Medical authorities tell us that practically all boys do it. No one knows for sure how many girls. Some couldn't care less. It isn't for them. Still some do, and I receive letters from both sexes. Some of those quoted above are from girls. They worry about it too. Yet, the majority of the ones who write me are quite within the range of normalcy.

All right, what's normal? That is the crucial question in many minds. Unfortunately, there is no quick answer because each body is different. So I would rather tell you about the bad and the good, then you decide for yourself.

■ *Masturbation has its negative side. It can be very bad.*

As in, "when?"

As when it is "compulsive-obsessive." The dictionary says that a compulsion is a "feeling of being irresistibly driven to the performance." Obsession is defined as "persistent preoccupation with an idea."

How that applies to masturbation is that you better be managing it rather than vice versa. If you let it control you, that's bad. If you side-step your difficulties rather than face up to them, that's bad. If you resort to self-solace when you need a firm hand, that's bad. If you go backward when you should go forward, that's bad.

Remember, the doctors said it is a natural part of *growing up*. Those last two words are the key. You be the one to decide. Do you think you are progressing naturally, growing up normally?

■ *It is important for you to understand fantasy.*

When I was a boy, an old doctor friend told me something that helped. He said, "You can never control who knocks on your door. What you can decide is who's coming in."

The truth is that most minds have some perfectly awful thoughts. Don't be surprised what comes knocking. You never need to be shocked at these things if you know how to chase them away.

Here are some test questions for judging: "Are my thoughts harmful to me or to others? Do I picture scenes of violence and over-aggression? Are my desires perverted, twisted, or way off the normal?"

Whatever you think, be honest! Evaluate the good and evil in you as openly as you can. Then, if it's just too much, take it to someone who can help you. But don't come unglued too soon.

■ *Masturbation can be a positive factor in your total development.*
This can be an important part, a very personal, strengthening part of your self-identity. To know that your system is capable of these amazing physiological reactions can be a good thing. This is especially true if you are a young teenager. You must learn to be grateful for your body and think of it as your friend.

Then too, masturbation can be a preventive to things getting out of hand. There is another old saying I learned in my teens. It helped me and I pass it along in the hope that it might help you. This is the word: "It is better to come home hot and bothered than satisfied and worried!"

So what does that have to do with masturbation? What it has to do with teenage masturbation is that teenage masturbation is preferable to teenage intercourse!

The chances are that you will need some release. Dates, dances, parties, swimming; riding in the car with a girl; watching this lovely thing walk down the hall; listening to a record; television; reading a book; thumbing through magazines—these all can turn you on. It would be a very unfortunate person who didn't have some sex feelings in today's sex-oriented society. So be glad you're that way. Accept yourself as you are. Then use the best brains you've been given to keep growing positively.

■ Which brings me to what I told my own children. What I taught them is that *masturbation is a gift of God.*

The Dignity of Your Own Judgment

What if the past generations had simply been blind to the truth? What if this was really the wise provision of a very wise Creator? What if He gave it to us because He knew we'd need it?

Let's not kid ourselves. Many of God's blessings become negatives when they are not used intelligently. But like so many other things it is really up to us. I told my children that *they* could make it evil or use it for good.

So that brings us to the crucial question. You know whether you want to be good. You know if you're sincerely interested in doing right. If you are, then this is the test for whether you're still with the healthy.

Question: ARE YOU EMBARRASSED ABOUT YOUR PERFORMANCE? IN YOUR OWN PRESENCE HOW DO YOU FEEL ABOUT YOU?

So long as masturbation is not humiliating, so long as it helps you to keep on the good side of sociable, so long as you can accept it as a natural part of growing up, then you thank God for it and use it as a blessing!

10

Doing Wrong in the Best Way

Put your ear down close now while I tell you a story. This is a true story. It happened just like I'm telling you. I know it did, so take it from me—this one's for real.

Once there were two parents who loved their children very much. There were several in the family with considerable age-spread.

This was an active family. They prayed together; worshiped together; worked together; had fun together; spent a lot of time together being a family. They also discussed things together so they came to know each other well.

This mother and dad believed in certain things. Important things, like:

Freedom of choice
> Accepting responsibility
>> Concern for others
>>> Respect for life
>>>> Love which keeps on loving

To live that way is a big order, as anyone can see. But they believed in it so they taught their children reverence for all these things. Naturally this wasn't easy. Sometimes they slipped and then they apologized. But everyone got the message and they worked at it together.

Now it happened that the two older children came to their teens at practically the same time. So the parents talked teen sex with them against the background of all I've been telling you. Actually, this was only one more step in their sex education. It started way back there.

Then one of their teenagers "fell in love." That's what she called it. The parents called it "growing up," only not to her they didn't. Like they thought, she was in and out of love that way several times.

But then came something different. This really *was* love and they knew that she knew. So now this mother and dad did an unusual thing. They sat down with their two teenagers and I will tell you what they said:

"You know we believe in you. We believe in your moral integrity. We respect your judgment. Since this is true, we want to give you some daring new thoughts. You know we think sex is what you would call 'heavenly.' In fact, we'll go you one better. We call it 'Divine!' Now here comes the important part. We think it can be more heavenly for you if you treat it with reverence. This means take it at the right pace. Get in step with the heavenly cadence. And that means wait for marriage!

"But whether you do or whether you don't is not our decision. It's yours. You have the right to do wrong sexually if you choose.

"So here's what we want to tell you: If you choose to do wrong, we hope you will do it in the best way for everyone concerned. What we mean here is—if you're going to have sex before marriage, for goodness sake, use birth control!

"We're not accusing you. But should the day ever come when the going gets rough, you come to us. If you want to marry early, we'll try to work it out. If you're not ready for that, then you be frank and we'll be honest.

"Well, that's about the size of it. Any questions? O.K. Meeting adjourned. Only there is one more thing: it takes some kind of great kids to trust them like this. Thanks."

What do you think? Too avant-garde? Asking for trouble? Encouraging wrong? Not the right method? There must be a better way?

I sure wish I knew one. So do a lot of teen strugglers who write me like this:

> Please help us. We vowed we never would, but we got carried away . . . Her parents found out and they threatened to break us up. But they never will. We belong to each other, all the way, every way . . . We are both very religious and we know it is wrong. We get down on our knees and promise we never will again. But then we do and we only feel worse . . . Don't tell us to stop because we're not going to . . . Sure we're taking chances, but whose business is that?

It's a lot of people's business, that's whose. It's parents' business, kinfolks'; friends' business, schoolmates'; church's business, society's. And it certainly can be ultra-bad business for the unborn baby. You can see how the list of the other people involved with another person's pregnancy goes on and on. I suppose it might be true, after the vows have been said, that what a married couple does with sex is their business. But that doesn't go for teen sex before they have been to the altar!

So, I think it is time for someone in our generation to say it plainly to your generation. Let's call this: TWO TRUTHS FOR UNMARRIED TEENAGERS ABOUT TO HAVE SEX.

■ *That boy who has intercourse without taking precautions is too irresponsible to deserve the name "father."*
■ *That girl who has intercourse without taking precautions is too irresponsible to deserve the name "mother."*

The facts are that too many babies are born out of wedlock. And too many others are born too early. And too many teens' lives get messed up too soon. Which means what? Which means somebody is having sex irresponsibly.

Babies come from intercourse, remember?

The stork is dead!

So, what can you do about it?

You can choose from many different methods of birth control: the pill, intrauterine devices (IUDs), a diaphragm, or condoms (ordinarily called "rubbers"). Vaginal jellies of many varieties are another option. The problem with birth control for many teenagers is that most of these methods need medical attention for proper use. And almost all forms of birth control are more effective with professional guidance.

If you will not go to a doctor, if you refuse to get help from someone who can guide you wisely, then go to the drugstore. Fast. For safety's sake, go together! Always, it is best for unmarried teenagers to have double protection.

Most boys know about male contraceptives. Any girl can find a variety of jellies, foams, or ointments for her use. Read labels and follow directions carefully. Here is the reason why I say both of you should use something. Doctors say condoms are only 80 to 90 percent effective. They also advise that female preventive methods are not much more than 90 percent certain. Looking at these two figures, you can see why double protection is important.

I simply do not see how I could make it plainer than that.

There are a couple of things *better* than that. One might be to call it quits, stop seeing each other.

Another is for you to have a solid fact-facing session with yourselves.

"Let's look at the facts, darling, all the facts. We know what our adult advisors think. Now what do *we* think? *We've* got to decide.

"We might quit going steady, date other people. Is that what we should do? It will take discipline. Do we have what it takes?

"We might never see each other alone. You know, double-date, only go to games, parties, wherever the gang is. But honestly now, how practical is that? Couples in love should be together alone.

"We might take the pledge. We will never, ever—swear on the Bible, raise your right hand—do it again! But what if we're fighting a losing battle? Is this a power greater than our own?" (I have known dozens of couples who knew they should quit; swore they would quit; claimed they had quit. But when the truth was out they couldn't.)

So, this is why I say: if you are having intercourse, sit down and have a deep-think session between you. Look at it this way. Look at it that way. Look at it from every viewpoint. Then, if you decide you can't quit, will you do this? Since you can't be as good as you wish, will you at least be as smart as you can?

If you have read this book carefully, you understand that I am not recommending premarital sex. Here it is again: I believe sex is a sacred gift of God. I believe it goes best for those who mark it "hold" and reserve it for marriage. I believe sex needs the sanctity of marriage and long-term commitment to make it what God intended.

But what *I* believe is not the most important item in your sexual decisions. You're the one who's going to have to make the final choices. That's why it's important that you think it through carefully and honestly.

A funny thing happens if you really will grow up that much. On the surface it looks like this would urge you on more often. But that isn't how it goes. An intelligent couple making an intelligent decision may experience this interesting reversal. What they have found is a new source of strength; a new regulator; new help for self-control.

Here is an interesting letter which shows clearly what I mean. I prize this letter because it is from two honest, let's-face-the-facts, all-American teenagers. They have written before and now comes this letter:

Dear Dr. Shedd:

We have a confession to make. We told you we were *thinking* about having intercourse. We asked your advice. The truth is we have been for several months, only we didn't even want to admit it to ourselves.

You really shook us with what you said about birth control. We acted real shocked. We pretended it was awful. Then we sat down and looked at each other. Right in the eye we did. And then we knew, both of us knew, we were being phoney. We decided you were right, and we have done what you said. We made a solemn pledge that we would never do it again without protecting both ourselves and everyone else who could be involved.

Only the thing which happened is that it is so much easier now to control. When we have to stop and get ready, this gives us time to think. It seems so serious, so businesslike, so unromantic. But one couple we know got pregnant and that sure isn't romantic either, is it?

11

Sex and the Mind Benders

I'm warning you, this is not a nice chapter. But I get so much mail of this kind I decided you ought to know. Sometimes life gets negative where sex is mixed up with artificial input, and this can be very very bad.

Like this:

This is from Ginny, who felt just awful . . .

All of a sudden I started to dance and everybody cheered only I don't remember what happened but my girl friend said I was really a mess. Then two of them took me down by the pond and tried to take my clothes off. One was holding me while the other was trying to make me be still. Then I kicked him and hurt him something awful. So they began slapping me because I wouldn't stop fighting. And they called me the most awful things. Then they went away. But my clothes were all torn when I got back and you know what they thought. Now they are telling all these awful stories. Dr. Shedd, what should I say? I feel just awful. Honest, I only had a few beers. Why didn't somebody tell me what it can do?

I'm sorry somebody didn't. But for those of you who don't know, I'm telling you now—the mind benders are foolers. Under their influence, you are probably getting dumber when you think you're getting smarter. Which, of course, is strictly no good for sex judgment.

From Terry, who couldn't remember the good part . . .

I have tried them all and have decided they are really nothing but a big gyp. The trouble is when it is over you can't remember the good part. At least I can't. All I have left is a headache or sick stomach or how dissatisfied I am after it wears off. So what have you got if you can't keep any of the good part?

What does this have to do with sex? Maybe a lot. Almost every good thing in life has these three parts: Anticipation, realization, memory! I can only ask you to believe me. In a great sex life, thinking back with pleasure is one of the great things.

From Beth, who felt so used . . .

The thing that I can't stand is thinking there are people like him who would do a person that way. How I know is that he blurted it out in the big fight when we broke up. He admitted he got me to drink on purpose. How could any boy be like that? I won't say we didn't have our good times. But now that it's over I feel so used.

Any man would be ashamed to admit that there are males like that. But there are. They invite you, they urge you. And then, when you have had too much, they use you. This is another bad thing about the mind benders. They have a way of transferring your controls into hands that aren't dependable.

From Jennifer, who doesn't know what happened . . .

The worst of it is this. We were both so high on the stuff we don't remember what all happened. I am so scared I can hardly write. What if we went all the way? What if I am pregnant? What can I do? He says he doesn't think we did, but I don't think he knows any more than I do. How could I be such a fool? As a matter of fact, I don't really care much about him. We were just going to try a little for kicks and now look. Do you think I am pregnant? Will I ever know for sure whether we did. It would be so terrible to always wonder. Please, can you help me remember?

No, I don't think she will ever know for sure. And no, I can't help her remember. I am sorry, but with some things no human being can help much. That's how the song goes, "You gotta walk that lonesome valley. You gotta walk this road alone." Which is another way the mind benders cheat you. They take away some things you wanted to keep. They might even give you some things you didn't want.

This is about Danny, whose "prognosis is somewhat unfavorable" . . .

This is a true story. I know because it happened in our neighborhood.

Danny is from an upper middle class home. His father is a prominent community leader. His mother is very nice. He wasn't the kind you expect to go berserk and he really didn't mean to. What happened was that he got into something he thought he could handle but it was too much for him.

I almost hate to tell you the next part. Today Danny is in a state hospital in Texas. His mind doesn't work right, his eyes won't focus, his speech is garbled. I don't like the way the doctors put it. They say it will take at least two years to be sure. Then there was one who told me, "The prognosis is somewhat unfavorable."

I feel sure that Danny was only experimenting. I am confident he never intended to get that much. I don't know whether it was just one time or if he kept going back.

But this is another place where the mind benders can tear you up. They might egg you on beyond your maximum. You know by now that sex is already one of life's strongest "come-on" emotions. Once it gets going, it provides its own urge. The further you go, the more you want. Without adding a thing you've got enough of that already. So you can see right away another problem with sex and the mind benders. They are not a good match. Two of these pushers inside you might overtax your judgment beyond its capacity.

THE STORK IS DEAD

We could go on and on. There are plenty more where these came from. Like I said, I really wish we might have skipped the whole thing. But the truth is there are some sinister influences around these days. Don't ever forget it.

Then there is one thing more you better do. It is a good idea, where sex is involved, to keep checking who's in control. Are you doing the thinking or is somebody else doing it for you? Do you really want to do this? Or are you doing it because somebody else is pressuring you?

One note that runs heavy through my letters is, "Why did I let them talk me into it?" You can immediately see how this could happen. At your age, approval is very important. You want to have friends, to please others, to be one of the gang. But you better believe it. Any place you go there are pushy, pushy people where sex is concerned. They would be delighted to take over your sex and manage it for you.

All of which brings us back where we've been before. Some things are yours, and yours alone, till you choose otherwise. That's why one of the most important questions you'll ever answer is this: "What will I do, and what will I not do, with the mind God gave me? Am I grateful enough for my ability to think?"

12

Ways to Handle Your Parents

Parents, parents! They are nothing but creeps. I hate my parents and so do most of my friends hate theirs . . . Please help me to get across to my dad that every boy isn't going to attack me. He is always cutting these terrible things out of the paper and putting them on my pillow. What is the matter? Is he some kind of sex nut? . . . My mom and dad make a federal case out of every date. You would think the boy was one of the FBI's "most wanted" or something . . . My mother is divorced and she says I can't date till I'm a senior. That will be two years. Do you think this is fair? . . . My parents make me come in every night by eleven. Even from the prom they do. But next year when I get to college, boy will I show them! . . . My folks are great in many ways but there is this wide gap between us and it is getting wider. . . .

These are exact quotations right out of my mail. And they feel so real, don't they? That's how it is. With you and your friends, that's how it is. Between parents and teenagers there are so many sore spots: Money, music, clothes, cars, hair, homework, friends, family (brothers, sisters, cousins, aunts, grandmas). In fact, almost any thing you mention could be another battleground.

But the leading call to arms is boys and girls together. Which means what? What it means is that you better watch it. You may begin acting out with other people how you feel toward your folks.

So, what does all this have to do with sex? Maybe we can get at it best by asking you something.

Question: What is one of the greatest things about sex?

Answer: PRIVACY!

Your sex is your own personal possession. This represents something which is very specially yours. It is a symbol of one place where the world won't intrude until you're ready.

Now, underneath all this teen-parent battle is what? Well, one answer is *the intrusion of privacy.*

You're growing up. You're feeling more and more capable of making your own decisions. You're pushing for independence. You're resenting restrictions. You're anxious to run your own life, manage your own schedule, pick your own friends, make your own rules.

That's how it is if you're normal. Your parents are providing your food, clothes, a roof over your head. So right now you can't be 100 percent independent from them.

There is one place, however, where you are in charge. This is your sexual activity.

Which is exactly what the girl means when she says: "But next year when I go to college, boy will I show them!"

There are many ways to say this and I've heard most of them: "I get *soo* mad!" . . . "It makes me *soooo* furious!" . . . "They think they are *soooo* smart!" But no matter how it's said, I always wince.

Why?

Because I also get letters like this: "Do you know why I did it? I did it to get even, that's why. And isn't that dumb?"

Yes, that's dumb. Whenever anyone uses sex to punish someone; or to strike back; or for any other reason than an expression of his best; that's dumb.

You have done yourself a big favor when you learn this truth so you'll never forget it: *Sex is one of life's most positive positives. To use it for negative reasons is strictly no good.*

Since this has happened, does happen, and could happen to you, think now. How can *you* help create a better climate between you and your parents? What are the secrets to healthier home relationships?

Some things can be done. Certain things will work. How do I know? Because they've been worked on me!

From what I've learned watching my own teenagers; from the ones I've seen who were getting the job done; from the letters I receive which seem to come from good backgrounds; I've put together these "Twelve Rules for Handling Your Parents." Why don't you think these through and then make up your own?

■ *Remember, you're no bargain to live with, either!*

If there is one thing tougher than being a teenager, it's having one. So when things get rough between you and your folks, suppose you go straight down the hall and look in the mirror. You've done a great thing for your future when you learn to *start* analyzing your people-conflicts with the question, "Where am I wrong?"

■ *Remember, nobody gets everything he wants, or everything she wants, either. There are other people in the world besides you!*

You're at the age when you begin wanting more. You want to try some new ideas, to feel more grown-up, to impress more people. But you better back off now and then to see the whole picture at your house and in the world. I do hope you get a lot of good stuff to live it up with. But don't forget the others—including your mom and dad—they like good stuff, too.

■ *Let them have their way sometimes, especially with the little things.*

The wise teenager doesn't try to win them all. There are dozens of small deals where it really doesn't matter who comes out on top. If you show them you are willing to give in a lot of the time, you're being smart. They are more likely to cooperate when it's some big deal you've just *got* to have. It is hard to turn down a teenager today who said yesterday, "I think you're right, dad. I hadn't thought of it like that." Learning to live with this kind of give-and-take is great for another reason. It is excellent preparation for life when you will be on your own.

THE STORK IS DEAD

■ *Show a little sympathy.*

One hundred percent of the time "understanding" is a good word for bettering any relationship. What it means is that you try to see things through the other person's eyes.

If you would make the effort you might find out some things about your folks. During your teen years it's possible your dad is having his toughest time ever. He's readjusting his thinking about how great he is. He's pulling down some of his goals. He's battling like crazy to keep his spirits up.

Your mother may be approaching the time of life which isn't easy for women. All kinds of fears and odd sensations go through some minds at middle age. Try really caring about how they feel. You'll be surprised! (We have this one character at our house who can get just about anything he wants. You know how he does it? When he comes home from school, he puts his arm around his mom and says, "Hi, baby, how'd it go today?" At night sometimes he sits by his dad and says, "You look tired, pop! Have a hard day?" This guy isn't a phony. He really does care. But I'm telling you true, when he asks for something, we have to be careful. We are tempted to give him the whole works.) Unless your parents are zombies, this kind of stuff is the greatest! "All God's chillun' got troubles these days"—including *your* mom and dad.

■ *Make a solemn vow: "I will say 'thank you' to each of my folks at least once every day."*

Go ahead. Of course, they'll fall flat on their faces, but they'll come out of it. And when they do, they'll be bragging everywhere about their wonderful teenager. Naturally, nobody will believe them. But they'll just *know* what an unusual child they have—which they do! A pat on the back is so unusual from someone your age that this can only work one way—positive. Appreciation always opens the door for good things later.

■ *At least once a week do something nice for your parents.*

It doesn't need to be something like buying a new car or paying off the mortgage. Any little thing will do so long as (a) they weren't expecting it, and (b) you get the message across that you'd like to make life a little easier for them. (I know one girl who, during her teen years, would say to her parents now and then, "This Friday I am going to stay home and baby sit. You're going out and have a good time." What do you suppose that did for their feelings toward her?)

■ *Learn how to say "I'm sorry."*

There is nothing, and I mean nothing, which marks you as a person of character like this. Discharging the obligation of your errors with an apology is big-time stuff. Of course, you're a stinker once in a while. We all are. And they'll be more prepared to make amends when *they* should if you do it when *you* should. Few things can lift the level of human relations like honest humility properly expressed.

■ *Never do anything to betray their trust or make them question your honesty.*

The first time you lie to your parents, you have put your foot on a treacherous road. It's all downhill from here. You'll never appreciate this till you are a parent: It is so great to *always* know that your children will tell you the truth. You can imagine how much easier it is to say "Yes" to someone like this. When your folks lose faith in you and it's *your* fault, you have lost a whole bunch. "Stupid" is the word for a teenage prevaricator.

■ *Try to work up agreements which will eliminate some arguments in advance.*

Use of the phone, for instance. Be reasonable—your folks do too have some friends, even if you don't see how anyone could stand them. You can settle some questions ahead of time. How often can you date? Who can you date? Where can you go? What time will you be in? How much allowance will you get? What work will you do around the house? How much privacy will they give you? How much will you give them in return? Dozens of these things can be agreed by prearrangement rather than fought over later. Smart teenagers think ahead!

■ *Ask their advice now and then on something big enough to make them feel important.*

There isn't a parent alive in sound mind who wouldn't react favorably to these four words: "I need your help!" If you would only come out from under your "dumb-parent" syndrome you might be surprised. They really *do* know some things worth knowing. And would they be flattered! And would that ever do something to improve the atmosphere around here!

■ *Tell them you'd like to know about sex straight from them.*

So, they were brought up in a day when things were different. But they must know a little, unless you really did come by stork. As I've said before, I honestly believe a whole lot of parents would like to *try*. If you'd only prompt them a little; or sit still long enough; or stay off the phone long enough; or show some open-mindedness long enough; or keep a straight face long enough; maybe they wouldn't do half bad. And the way I'd begin would be something like this: "I want you to be proud of me. I know you're a lot smarter than some of the sex-sources around here. Please, will you answer some questions for me?"

■ *Communicate! Oh, go on, please try! Please, just one sentence now and then.*

The truth is that, communication-wise, the average teenager is simply awful. Many a home hears only one sound from teen lips: "Uh!" Of course, sometimes it is said double—"Uh! Uh!"—which, being interpreted, means the opposite. You better believe me, that's about the worst thing in the world for a parent to live with. So quit grunting and begin communicating. Here's a rule that simply can't miss. Every day put together one sentence and every week one paragraph. Life will be a whole lot more bearable if you do.

"But it's no use! My folks *are* impossible!"

So?

So, I'm sorry.

But then there was this one boy who wrote:

I was thinking all these horrible thoughts about my parents when suddenly it hit me—If they're all that bad, how come I'm so wonderful?

13

Forgiveness and the Road Back

(Letter from teen girl.)

Dear Dr. Shedd:

Thank you for your articles in *Teen*. After reading them, my boyfriend and I had a long talk and we decided to break up. This was the hardest thing we ever had to do up till now, but we both knew it was right. We aren't old enough yet to be sure about so many important things. One thing we aren't sure about is whether anybody can be mature enough to be completely in love at 16, which is my age, and 17, his age.

But the thing which bothers us is that we have been doing things which are wrong and we both know it. We didn't want to, but it just happened because we were together all the time.

What bothers me now is how I can ever stand before the altar on my wedding day and feel right. Do I have a right to wear a white dress like I always dreamed? Do you think I will be forgiven?

B. J.

Dear B. J.

If there were prizes for teenage maturity, I would nominate you and your boyfriend. One sure sign of real maturity is knowing where you are not mature enough yet. You are both to be congratulated. I think you're great.

Thank you also for sharing your wrong with me. I want you to feel now that you have put it where it belongs by giving it to me. You ask whether you can ever be as good again as you were before this happened. The answer is that you can be not only as good but you can actually be a finer person than you were. Our religion teaches us that God forgives us totally if we come in genuine penitence with a sincere promise to live up to our best in the future.

Right away somebody is going to jump on that with a question—"If this is true, why not do wrong so we can be forgiven?" The Bible has some very pointed things to say about this tricky maneuver. What it says is that this is phony and God can spot a phony every time.

But when we face up to our wrongs, when we are sincerely sorry, then He has a wonderful way of taking these things and using them. He uses them by working them into the fabric of our lives to make us finer, lovelier, more complete people.

With the spirit you now have, you can be a more sympathetic, more understanding, more beautiful person for the rest of your life.

So don't punish yourself with guilt. God doesn't want you to do that. You go on loving life and people in the right way, and I say it's a lucky boy who is going to get somebody like you. If I know what the mercy of God means, then you go on being as honest and sincere as you are now; and when you stand there in your white wedding gown, you will look perfectly beautiful to that boy and to the God whose mercy is greater than our wrongs.

This is what forgiveness means in religion, and it is great, good news, isn't it!

Sincerely,
Dr. Shedd

III

Etcetera

In this section I am sharing with you excerpts from letters I have received. These were chosen from my files because they deal with things I think you should know. In each Etcetera the first part is from a teenager. My answer begins with the second part.

Etcetera Number 1

"Please Help Me. I Think I'm Pregnant."

Please help me. I think I am pregnant. I am two months late for my period and I never have been before. What can I do? I am afraid to tell my parents. It will just kill them, especially mom. Do you know any homes where I could go? What about abortions? I heard about this one girl who had one and she almost died. Please help me. I don't know what to do.

I'll tell you exactly what to do, and I hope you'll do what I tell you. First, you have one of two choices:

(1) Go right now to your parents. Sure it will crush them, but it won't kill them like you say. After the first shock is over you may be surprised how they will be. They're going to find out some time. Since you can't think for yourself, try to believe me. The sooner your parents know it from you, the better they will take it.

(2) Go at once to your doctor. He's the only one who can tell for sure. He can. also advise you about homes for unwed mothers. Ask him your questions about abortion.

Whichever of these you choose, the second step follows: If you go first to your folks, they'll take you to the doctor. If you go first to your doctor, you must then go to your folks. What you need is support. You need some adult thinking. Next, there is one thing I would *not* do and one more thing I would try.

I would not tell anyone. I know girls who ran frantically from friend to friend and later were sorry. That I would not do.

The thing I would try is this: I would try to think positively about my future. I hope you have a minister you like. If you do, I'd go to him and listen to the good news of God's forgiveness. Then I would work real hard to be forgiving toward others and toward my self.

It is very important that you learn to think well of you once more. I know girls who kept putting themselves down until they made a second serious mistake. They had so little self-respect left they wanted to be sure they were still lovable. As a result they became sexually involved again.

But you have had enough bitterness. You must train yourself to think well of you, of marriage, of men, of sex. Life can be wonderful again. Everything you've learned can help you. You can be wiser, more understanding, more ready to live, more ready to love.

Etcetera Number 2

"I Am So Mixed Up about Abortion"

I am so mixed up about abortion. I am pregnant and my boyfriend says there is only one thing for me to do. He wants me to get an abortion right away. This really bothers me. I am a very religious person and here I am trying to decide whether I should take my own baby's life.

Should I go through this pregnancy, and if I do, could I even think of giving my baby up for adoption? Or what if I kept the baby, how would I ever manage?

My parents have promised to stand beside me, whatever I decide. But they both have to work, so how could they help care for a baby?

Sometimes I agree with my boyfriend that abortion would be the easiest answer, but then I ask myself how I will feel about this a long time from now.

Do you think abortion is ever right?

Most adults would agree that there are times when abortion might be the preferable choice. In cases of rape, danger to the mother, or possible damage to the baby due to medication or sickness, that could be the answer. But these are not your problems.

You are asking me what I think. So, first, I am glad you are religious, because I believe your struggle is theological; a great many Christians believe that a baby is a child of God at the moment of conception.

Second, I think you are right in insisting that *you*—and not your boyfriend—make your decision. My advice to you is to carry the baby through these nine months and then give it up for adoption. That will be hard, but you will be giving your child a chance to grow up in a home where he or she is wanted. And you will also be helping some childless couple who might otherwise never have a son or daughter.

One of the great facts of our faith is that God can turn things that seem so awesome and awful into a miracle if we give him a chance.

I hope as you continue praying for God's guidance you will hear some clear answers. I will pray for you, too.

Etcetera Number 3

"Do You Think I Should Force Him to Marry Me?"

I'm pregnant and now Freddy says he isn't sure any more. He swore that he loved me. You should have heard him. Only now he acts so funny. I don't know what to do. Do you think we should get married? Will he start loving me again when the baby comes?

Don't count on it. He may even hate you if you force him to marry you. The reason? You have taken away his freedom. He sees himself in jail and you as the jailer. He wants to be free to have fun. He wants to go places, do things, get an education, follow a career.

So, is this fair? No, it sure isn't, but it's real.

I'm sorry for you, honest I am. I'm so very sorry for you. But I'm also sorry for a lot of other people. I'm not out to make you feel worse than you already feel. But I am saying, "You must grow up fast. You must try hard to see the total picture. You must ask yourself what is best for everyone under all the circumstances? What's best for the baby's future; for Freddy's; for yours? What's best for both families; your parents; Freddy's parents; brother, sister; uncles and aunts? What's best for the school; your friends; society? Try hard to take this big a look. You owe so much to so many."

Do I think you should get married? No. It takes many things to make a marriage. One thing it takes is two people who want very much to get married. There is no other basis for a good marriage than love from both sides.

Etcetera Number 4

"What Do They Mean by 'Making Out'?"

What do they mean by "making out?" I hear them talking about this and I am confused over what they mean.

So am I. The problem is that meanings vary from school to school. They also differ from region to region, from teenager to teenager.

When I was a boy there was this game called "postoffice." It was a kissing game but not very heavy. "Smooching" was our label for the sloppier stuff.

Every age has its own terminology. But when anyone in your crowd talks about "making out," you better understand there is a wide range. For some it has the most innocent meanings. To others this is the term for the complete sex act.

Etcetera Number 5

"Why Do Boys Tell So Much?"

Why do boys tell so much? He said all these beautiful things and now do you know what happened? He's telling all over school. I am so embarrassed I could just die. How can he be like that?

There are several reasons why boys do this. For one thing, they take sex much more casually than you do. Sure, they may give you all kinds of assurance. But they can toss that off lightly too even if you can't. Then, males like to think of themselves as "collectors." They often brag about their conquests to impress themselves and other males.

But probably the hardest thing to take is right here: He can talk like that because he has lost respect for you. A part of him scorns you. He sees you now as "Damaged Goods." Since you didn't think highly of yourself, he sees no reason why he should.

There is a sad verse in the Bible which reads: "The hatred with which he hated her was greater than the love with which he had loved her." It's been this way for a long time.

Etcetera Number 6

"What Do They Mean by Erogenous Zones?"

What do they mean by erogenous zones?

This means areas which are particularly sensitive to sex stimulation. Normally the number one areas are the genitals (girl's vagina, boy's penis). Others are breasts, nipples, ear lobes, neck, parts of the back, even the feet. The tongue and mouth can become erogenous zones very quickly. This is the reason behind what you call "French kissing."

There is nothing sinful about erogenous zones. To have some and know what they are is not wrong. What you do with them could be. So, you are wise if you decide some things right now. You can determine ahead of time what you will do and what you will not do. If you do this, your erogenous zones can be your friends. They will protect you if you let them.

Where I live, every now and then we have "storm warnings." They come by radio, television, newspaper. When we get the word, we can take necessary precautions. We can also decide to get away from here fast if that's best. Sometimes those who refuse to pay attention are sorry afterwards.

If you listen, your body will do you like that. Most people are equipped with danger signals. Naturally these will be different with different bodies, but yours will serve you well if you let them. As you become expert in reading the warnings, you will gain more confidence. You will also be a safer person both for yourself and other people.

Good luck. I hope that at the right time with the right person you will learn this: *Your body is very wonderful, including its erogenous zones.*

Etcetera Number 7

"Will You Tell Me What Is a 'Climax'?"

I hear them talking about "climax." I also saw it in a paperback book. I don't think I ever had one. Will you please tell me what they mean?

This is the high point of sexual intercourse. All pre-intercourse play (petting, fondling, stroking) is moving toward this end.

It is a wonderful inner explosion of pleasure. It begins with a warm sensation in the body; this builds into a mounting urgency; then it intensifies in the sex organs; then it "comes" in a gentle-to-violent release which brings physical ecstasy.

This is the origin of the word "coming," so commonly used among teenagers. "Orgasm" is another term for the same thing. A "climax" can also take place from petting or through masturbation alone.

Etcetera Number 8

"He Says We Should Try It to See if It Fits."

He says we should try it to see if it fits.

Shades of the lines guys use! This one we can call, "variation on an old theme." Other versions go, "How do we know we're mated unless we do it?" . . . "I wouldn't marry any girl until I knew for sure we were the right size for each other."

So, where else is the guy all wrong? Doctors say that size is no test for true love. They also say that many happy marriages involve sex organs of considerable divergence. This is true because the vagina has an amazing elasticity. But there is a catch to this. Female reaction depends on many things including what's in the mind. If a woman is worried or hurried, if she is doubtful, her whole being may "tighten up."

This is one more reason why sex at its best needs marriage. It also explains why some girls feel nothing but pain without that protective permanence.

Whenever you hear this pitch, mark this guy down for stupid. Either he doesn't know or he's trying to win on a falsehood. This is a good time to say, "Listen, Junior. You don't need sex from me. You need information. Stay tuned, big boy! I am about to tell it like it is . . ."

Etcetera Number 9

"Sometimes a Boy Wants the Girl To Turn Him Down."

I think a girl should know that sometimes a boy wants to get turned down. Let me tell you what I mean. My girl finally gave in and it seems like I liked her better when she wouldn't.

I think what happened is it was nice to dream about how it would be when we got married. Now I don't dream any more and no matter how hard I try I can't make myself feel about her like I used to. I may still marry her but I am wondering if I wouldn't admire a girl better and love her more if she wouldn't let me.

I think another thing is I lost my sense of pride. I used to congratulate myself on how I could keep my self-control. Now I can't. Sure I like it, but it really isn't all that great that you should think less of yourself, is it? Why don't you tell the girls they may be taking something very nice away from the same guy they think they are being nice to.

There is an age-old question which goes "Why do men play around with girls who will and marry girls who won't?"

One answer is that they want a life-mate who brings out their best. Here is a wonderful letter about that. It is from a Minnesota mother who wrote it for girls everywhere. She sent it asking if I could use it in one of my columns. I'm glad to pass it along because I think it is loaded with wisdom.

Dear teenage daughters:
You are asking, "Why should I save myself for marriage?" I wish I could get you to back off long enough to think of what might be good for the boy in his total development.
What if he needed something more than he needed sex and you had a chance to give him this one thing and you didn't do it? One thing every man needs is strength. Strong men are not those who have always gotten what they want. The truly happy man is one who is developing his inner strength. He does this largely by self-control and he must do it if he is to be successful.
As a mature woman, you will want a mature mate. If this boy is the right one, then you want him to be the greatest man he can be. You want him to be strong in every way. Wouldn't it be too bad for you both if you weakened him by saying "Yes" when you might have made him better for the future by saying "No"?
There is an old line I have read often in advice columns to teenage girls. It is that she should say, "If you really loved me, you would want to protect me." How about turning that around and saying to him, "Because I love you, I want to protect *you*. I want to help you grow. I think I can help you more by not giving in."

Minnesota Mother

Etcetera Number 10

"Quality Is More Important Than Quantity."

Some of the fellows laugh at me because my penis is so small. It really isn't very big. Do you think this will make any difference?

You would be surprised how many boys are anxious about this. Usually these are in the younger age group, sometimes slow developers, worried too soon. But I also hear from older teenagers who think their sexual equipment is too small. So, I'm glad you wrote because I can see how this would bother you.

The truth is that pleasing a woman has little to do with the size of the male organ. The idea that it has to be big is based on false information. Much of this comes from pornography. That means books of wild sex stories, or pictures which leave the wrong impression. They tell tall tales about women who went wild because he was so large. This is mostly fantasy, not reality. Many a man with a small penis is "the most" sexually to his wife.

With a lot of things quality is more important than quantity. This is one of those places.

Etcetera Number 11

"I Never Had a Wet Dream."

I am awful worried. I have never had a wet dream. There are these three of us who go around together all the time. What bothers me is both my friends have had wet dreams and I never have. Everything else seems O.K. Do you think there might be something wrong with me?

No! Don't let it bug you. This is a common teenage worry, but it shouldn't be. Some boys never have "nocturnal emissions" and they get along fine. There are several reasons why you may be different from your friends. Maybe you're not built like they are. Your system doesn't need wet dreams. Maybe you'll have them later. Maybe you masturbate enough to rid your body of the buildup which wet dreams are really for. But I can assure you lots of sexually virile men never had wet dreams.

Etcetera Number 12

"I Do Not Feel Like Making Passes."

Sex doesn't seem as important to me as it does to the other guys. I like a lot of girls and especially this one. I go over to her house and we sit around listening to records. We also enjoy talking. But I never feel like making passes or things like that. This bothers me. Some of my friends talk about making out. I don't even want to. Am I all right, do you think? I forgot to tell you I am high point man on our basketball team.

Maybe I can help you by telling you about two young people I know. Neither of them came alive sexually until they were out of their teens. One of these is a boy with an avid interest in his special hobby. The other is a girl who came to me considerably worried. It troubled her that she was never sexually excited during her engagement. But both of them are happily married. They tell me life is great for them in every way. If you could see them with their mates, I'm sure you would believe what they say.

Teenagers don't all mature at the same pace. You might even be grateful if you are one of these. As long as you enjoy being with girls; as long as you think you are coming along naturally in other interests; I wouldn't worry yet.

Etcetera Number 13

"You Should See This Girl in Our School. Wow!"

This girl in our school wears clothes that really turn a fellow on. Only none of the guys can get to first base with her. You should see her! Wow! Don't get me wrong. I am just wondering, that's all.

Are you sure that's all? Don't start kidding yourself at this age. If she excites you sexually, admit it. It's the things we won't face up to that hurt us later. But you are real smart to figure this out. With some girls, sexy dress is the only sexy thing around. Low necklines, tight blouses, hip-hugging skirts might be foolers.

Sometimes when this gets out of hand it is called "exhibitionism." It is one of the strange twists sex takes when it is unhealthy. There are many of these quirks. You can read about them in good sex education books from your library. I urge you to learn what you need to know from authoritative sources.

But you can count on this—whenever there is enough gap between "different" and "normal" to attract excessive attention, something is wrong inside. This girl may be wearing her problems. By her clothing, her hairstyle, her makeup, she is displaying her neuroses to the world.

One thing is almost certain. She feels inferior. What she wants is not sex, but attention. A girl who is "just right" in appearance indicates a healthy climate inside. She knows that good taste is the most attractive in the long run. We call this "discreet." Your crowd calls it "couth." But whatever the name, it is the mark of a true lady, and very important.

Etcetera Number 14

"Can a Nymphomaniac Be Cured?"

What is a nymphomaniac? One of my girl friends told me that is what the whole school is calling me. I don't know for sure if that is what I am but if I am, I want to know can a nymphomaniac be cured? I don't want to be this way, but I just go out of my mind when I am with a boy. Only the strange thing is I don't really enjoy it and I never have. Each time I am more ashamed than ever. Then when I get over that, or when I meet a new boy, I get these feelings again. It is awful to be like this. I have even thought about killing myself. Won't you please try to help me before something terrible happens?

First, I want to say that you sound to me like a basically worthwhile person. It is always great to meet someone as honest as you are. You have the first two requirements for a cure. One is to admit you have a problem and the other is to want help. But you must now take step three, which is to go immediately to a doctor. Tell him your troubles. If he can't help you, he will know someone who can.

Nymphomania is curable. Whether this is the right word for you is not for me to judge. It means "morbid uncontrollable sexual desire in a female." It usually comes from deepseated emotional entanglements in the subconscious. But I feel sure you can be helped because of your attitude. And when you are better, I know you'll be an extra-fine person.

Etcetera Number 15

"He Gets a Strange Pleasure from Hurting Me."

I am engaged to be married but I am beginning to wonder. Last night Denny hurt me again. He bent my hand back when we were at the show and I almost screamed out loud. He has done this several times before. Once he pinched me so hard at a party it left a mark for days. It seems so peculiar because it never happens unless we are with other people. It is as though he gets a strange pleasure from hurting me.

I never know for sure when it is going to happen or why he does it. He hardly ever apologizes, but he usually promises he won't do it again. What do you think I should do? Will he get over this?

The term for this is "sadism." The dictionary defines it as a sexual perversion in which the torturer gets satisfaction from hurting the loved one. This is something beyond your ability to handle. He obviously needs professional help. Unless he gets it, your marriage would probably be a real torture chamber. I hope you can get him to see a psychiatrist. And if you decide to marry him as he is now, I hope *you* see a psychiatrist.

Etcetera Number 16

"Why Does My Dad Read
All These Terrible Things?"

Why does my dad read all these terrible things? For a long time now I have known about it. One day I accidentally found out where he hides them. You wouldn't believe what is in them. I have been looking in there for several years when he is gone from home and it seems they are getting worse. Lately, I even found some objects that are very queer. I have never told my mother because she is not very well and is such a sad person already. The only one I have told is my girl friend. She says she heard all men are that way. Are they really? I wonder if she knows because her mother and father are separated. If that is true, I don't think I ever want to get married. I would be horrified if my husband ever treated me like they do in those books and in the pictures.

You must think I know something or you wouldn't have written me. So I hope you will believe what I'm going to say. It could be very important to your future.

Most men are curious about sex, but it is a healthy curiosity. But your father is one of those unfortunate men with an insatiable curiosity problem. The reason why things are getting worse is this: He keeps looking for worse and worse stories and pictures to satisfy him. But, "insatiable" means "incapable of being satisfied." It is a pitiful condition, because men like this wouldn't know satisfaction if they found it. So, don't blame your mother. If I were you I wouldn't tell her. She may already know and that may be why she is sad.

The truth is she can't do anything for him; you can't do anything for him; he is the only one who could do anything.

His problem probably goes way back to his early life. It is not incurable but first he would have to want help. I am sorry this has happened to you. But I am even sorrier for your father and mother. Try to be as kind to them as you can be. They need it.

If you will let it, this can help you be a more understanding person. That will make you more attractive to some healthy boy. I hope some day you will marry a man who can teach you how fine sex can be.

When this subject came up in a recent teen workshop, an unusual thing happened. A mature high school senior asked for the floor and gave us this report:

When I read that story in *The Stork is Dead,* I could hardly believe it, because the same thing happened to me. I found all this strange stuff in the trunk of my father's car. I thought about it a long time and finally decided I would talk to him. Sure, I was scared, but what I did was to take him some of these things and told him I thought this was weird and he should get help. Do you know what? He didn't get mad like I thought he would, and I think the reason is he was glad somebody would talk to him. Anyway I can tell you he started going to a counselor and I think he may be getting some better. I can't tell how good this makes me feel and I decided maybe I should tell about it so anyone else who has problems like this with their parents would know sometimes there is something you can do even if it is hard.

Etcetera Number 17

"Boys Turn On Easier But They Turn Off Harder."

The most terrible thing has happened. I could just die. Donald has been like a brother to me. He said he told me for my own good, and

I suppose he did. But what he said was that all the boys are saying these awful things about me. I don't mean about going all the way because I wouldn't. But it's all this terrible stuff about being a teaser. Do you know what I mean? Some of them are so terrible I wouldn't even put them on paper. Honest, I could just die.

Sure I like to flirt. I get a big kick out of boys noticing me. I also like to make out up to a point. But believe me, I never did go all the way. So I don't think this is fair, do you? What can I do? I could just die.

Yes, I know what you mean. When I was a teenager, we had our own names for this kind. They weren't very nice either. I guess that's how it will always be. In every generation, boys will hate girls who seem to promise what they won't deliver.

There is a reason for this. It is a special male reason. How it goes is: *Boys turn on easier than girls, but they turn off harder!* This is why a smart girl will learn to say "No" long before things reach fever pitch. Unless she intends to give him what he's after, she isn't playing fair.

Do you suppose what is hurting you most is that you know you have been overdoing? Some times when "I could just die," it is because I am ashamed of me. But this kind of thing usually isn't fatal. Particularly, it isn't if I admit I was wrong.

If I were you, I would do that and lower the thermostat. I'll bet it won't be long till you and the boys have both cooled down to a more comfortable temperature.

Etcetera Number 18

"Everybody Laughs If You Have Good Morals."

You wouldn't believe the awful things that go on in our school. All the kids in our class think about is going somewhere and making out. Everybody just laughs at you if you have good morals. So what can a person do?

Let me tell you a funny thing that happened recently. There was this church meeting where sixty-three young people were present. One boy went home and told his mother, "nobody comes any more." How I know is because she told me. What happened? You know. None of his buddies showed up.

Anyone who works with teenagers learns to discount their exaggeration. I'll bet you're overdoing it for emphasis. Do you really mean "all the kids" and "everybody"? I'm sure there must be some of the good guys around there. Maybe you haven't looked hard enough in the right places.

Besides, what if everybody does do it? Character is partly guts enough to stand up for what *you* think is right. So don't let them wear you down. One day you'll be glad you lived up to your best even if your whole school is as bad as you say.

One more thing. Exaggeration is sometimes a sign that something is bugging you. Fantasies, morbid curiosity, undue excitement about the sins of others, are often tell-tale indicators.

I am not asking you to condone evil. What I am asking is that you check this question: Are you sounding these alarm notes out of some neurotic crack in your own makeup?

Etcetera Number 19

"Is It Really Safe If We Do It This Way?"

We have been having relations for six months and I never got pregnant. Billy takes it out just before he comes and he says this is perfectly safe. Only I will tell you something that bothers me. My girl friend got pregnant. She said they did it that way too and now look at her. So I am worried but he says not to be. Is it really safe if we do it this way?

No! "Coitus interruptus" is not safe! This is the technical term for "withdrawal" and it is as old as the Bible. But you are very unwise to depend on it. Billy may believe what he tells you. But you both should know that sperm are terrific movers. They are lightning swift. Ejaculated anywhere near the vagina they can make their way in. Also during the sex act some sperm might escape before full climax. Then, what if one time he got carried away and forgot?

The fact that you have gone like this six months doesn't make it safe. You may have been lucky. It only takes once, and remember, *you are never a little bit pregnant.*

You know from what you have read that I do not believe in sex before marriage. But I can't stop you. If you decide to continue, then please consider your total responsibility. Society, your parents, friends, your own future! These all might have to pay for your carelessness. This is why I say—if you are going to do wrong then do it in the best way! You aren't doing that now!

Etcetera Number 20

"Why Do You Protestants Believe in Birth Control?"

I am a Catholic engaged to a Protestant. We are both very religious. We are going to be married next spring and we get along so well except about birth control. We argue over it all the time. I have told him what our church permits but he says it isn't good enough because his sister married a Catholic and she got pregnant right away. He says he doesn't want to have a baby so soon because he has two more years of college and then law school. Then it takes a long time to get started after that.

I can see how he feels because I am going to work so he can finish. We have argued about it so much we avoid the subject now but we both know we will have to decide something before the time comes. One of my friends who works in the same factory with me has a priest who told her she should make up her own mind. I was brought up very strict and don't know if I should. Suddenly, while I was reading one of your columns I decided maybe it would help if I asked you to explain why Protestants believe in birth control. I have never heard it explained by a Protestant minister. Mark said he never had either. We both thought it would be a good idea because we just keep going over the same old points.

I forgot to tell you we are both nineteen. Our folks are all for us but they have different ideas too since they are both very strong in their own churches. We will appreciate any help you can give us.

You sound like a wonderful couple. I would like to help but before we talk about birth control, let's look at something else. You and Mark need to face up to one basic difference in your churches. You say that you had a strict Catholic training. Then you may have been taught that the Church decides what is right and wrong. Mark, as a strong Protestant, has been taught something else. He was trained to think the Church exists to help *him* decide what is right. That is a very important difference. What you need to determine is the answer to this question: "Can God, as we understand Him out of our different backgrounds, speak to us together?" As a Protestant minister, I feel this is your only hope.

The most successful Catholic-Protestant marriages I know are like this: They have created a Church in their hearts together! This is their real Church. Their other two churches are for the purpose of strengthening this Church in their home. If you and Mark can do that, then I see your marriage as hopeful. If you can't, I think you would each be better off married to one of your own faith. Your religion means too much to each of you to weaken it in any way. If you can strengthen it together, then you will really have a great thing.

With that as a background I can now tell you why Protestants believe in birth control. Perhaps it would be fairer for me to say, "Here is why *this* Protestant believes in birth control." In light of our "think for yourself" training, no Protestant can speak for all the others. But I believe these reasons are a fair summary of what most Protestants believe.

1. *We believe that God gave us the sex act for many reasons.* The creation of children is only one of these. Others are two people enjoying God's gift together; the spiritual union of two souls expressing their love to each other; the physical and emotional well-being of both individuals; the strengthening of the marriage vows through frequent coming together; rest; joy; fun; excitement; cleansing of minds and hearts; and other things too numerous to mention. Birth control makes these blessings possible more often.

2. *Complete freedom from fear is important to full expression in the sex act.* A woman, subconsciously worried about pregnancy, may hold back more than she should. This may be a deterrent to her total enjoyment. It may also cause the husband to feel that something is lacking. Sexual intercourse combines both relaxation and abandon when it is right. We hold that birth control contributes to sex as it was intended by its Creator.

3. *Planned parenthood makes better sense.* Spacing children is wiser than having them as they happen. We believe this is true attention-wise, money-wise, room-wise, education-wise and almost every-wise. It seems to us that planned families have a better chance of being happy families.

4. *The mother's health is all-important.* Having children too close is not good for a woman. Emotionally and physically the demands of her life can be better handled if she is in top condition. If she feels better, her husband will. This is one more reason why we believe planned parenthood is right.

5. *Adjusting to each other is important before a third party comes into the picture.* There are so many little things to be worked out between you. To work these out without interruption may be very necessary. One or both of you may need full attention at first. This,

of course, is one of the saddest things about having to get married. Many couples, denied that first time together alone, have paid for it in heartache later.

6. *Sexual frustration needs to be cleared in early marriage.* People like you come to the altar with a lot of self-denial in your background. This is admirable and we are glad you have high morals. But when it becomes legal you need to enjoy what you have been waiting for. It is true that you can still have intercourse during pregnancy. But no couple's sex life can be at its best during this period. You should be free to empty the storehouse of restraint. It will make you better people in the future. (Once I conducted a personal experiment in counseling. Whenever I had a case where the husband was unfaithful I inquired about the marriage circumstances. It was amazing how many of these men had to get married. I couldn't help asking myself this question: "Do you suppose he didn't get all the sex he needed in their early marriage?")

Like I said, these are just a few reasons. I hope they will help you toward a wise decision. But don't ever forget this: What you think doesn't matter nearly so much as what you think God thinks! You should love each other so much that you want this above all else for each other—*Perfect harmony between me and my friend and God!*

Etcetera Number 21

"I Am Worried about Catching a Venereal Disease."

Maybe I am being silly but I am worried about catching a venereal disease. I read in a book that you can get it off a toilet. My girl friend says the only way is from having intercourse with a boy. I don't want you to think I have it because I have never done it, but it still worries me a lot. Also, can you catch it from drinking glasses and from kissing a boy? I hope you won't think I am silly, but it would help me to know some of these things.

Concern about venereal disease is natural at your age. Since I am not an M.D., I called my doctor and read him your letter. This is what he said: "The transference is almost always by intercourse."

That's what he said and I trust his judgment. I hope you have a doctor you can go to with confidence. He might give you some good material to read on venereal disease. Generally, doctors like to help teenagers and are very wise in their counsel. You can also get information at most public health centers. Chances are good that your library has some dependable reading on this subject. Remember: "It's your head, and what's in it is your responsibility."

Etcetera Number 22

"Should We Get Married Just Because?"

Should a girl marry the boy just because he was the first one? Tom and I have gone together for two years and we have done things we shouldn't. But lately I am beginning to wonder. I think I may be falling out of love. One thing is this other boy who is my lab partner. He is so nice and he has asked me to go out.

Tom and I always talked about getting married. He still wants to but I am not sure. Only he says any good girl should marry the boy she has had relations with. I always thought it was for marriage too, but I honestly believed we would get married. Please help me to think straight about this. I am getting so confused.

It is obvious that Tom is trying desperately to hold you. I don't blame him because you sound like a very sensitive girl.

I am not going to judge you. Your own conscience has already done that. But you still want a reply to your question. So here is my answer: I think the boy a girl marries should be the first one. But, if that is no longer possible, if the facts are that there isn't a first time left, if she is "falling out of love," then she should not marry a boy *just because* he was the first one. A good marriage needs more behind it than that.

Etcetera Number 23

"What Will My Husband Think?"

I know it was wrong so please don't scold me. I feel bad enough already. Only do you know what bothers me most? What will my husband think? Do I have to tell him?

When the time comes you'll know whether you ought to tell. Every person is different and so is the one you will marry. If I were you, I wouldn't try to decide this now.

Some counselors say, "Never talk about your past." I don't agree. That may be the best advice for some and the very worst for others. Of course, you will see the wisdom of deciding before marriage. If you are not going to tell, then you should both agree ahead of time. You should work out some kind of pledge which says: "We will put our two pasts behind us. We will not mention them again until we *both* agree that we should change this pledge."

Some women I know waited till after marriage and then told. Some of these were sorry they did. Others developed such confidence in their husband's love that they wanted to tell. And I know several who said they found a new freedom in this sharing. They were hung up until they got rid of what bothered them. With a conscience like yours, you may be like that.

From what I have seen in marriage counseling, I think the long-range goal should be total knowledge. I have known many marriages which failed for lack of total sharing. I can't think of any which broke up from sharing too much.

Great marriage is one total person loving another total person. This means you love your mate for what he is now. You love him for what he will be in the future. But you also love him for what he's been through. You love his heartaches, his agonies, his sins, his whole being. If you love a man that much, chances are he will love you that much in return. Same too from him to her.

So don't worry at this stage. If you meet the right boy, you can tell him. You can tell him all about you and he will love you more for telling. He might even have a few things to tell you.

Etcetera Number 24

"My Husband Says I'm Not a Virgin."

My husband says I am not a virgin because I didn't have what he calls a "maidenhead," or something like that. He keeps after me all the time to tell him about where I lost it, who I had intercourse with, and things of that kind. Honest, Dr. Shedd, I never had relations with anyone but him. What can I do?

He is talking about the "hymen" which is a thin-to-heavy shield over the vaginal entrance in some women. The Bible refers to it and certain societies consider it all-important. But these are generally what we call "primitive" people.

Most doctors will tell you this is no test for virginity. A girl can lose it without ever knowing it happened. This may take place early in childhood. It might have broken when she was bicycling, riding horseback, or in some other way. More likely it was so thin she never felt it.

Doctors tell me some girls are even born without a hymen. For a nineteen-year-old wife you're going to have to take a firm hand. Tell him to get off this kick and stay off it. Ask him to go to a doctor who can explain it to him. If this doesn't do it, he'd better see a psychiatrist. Men sometimes "project" their guilt. That means he could be pointing at you to get the monkey off his back. We'll hope it is just ignorance on his part. But whatever it is, you might ask him to think about this: In the best kind of marriage a husband loves his wife for what she *is*, not for what she has done.

Etcetera Number 25

"What Is the Truth about Adultery and Fornication?"

My boy friend says adultery is sex with a married person and that is what the Ten Commandments forbid. He says if we had it, that would be fornication and it isn't so bad. But I can't help wondering. I have tried to find the answer in my Bible, but I can't. I also looked it up in the dictionary and it doesn't help either. Can you tell me what is the truth?

You're a smart girl. Sex-hungry boys are not exactly the highest source of biblical scholarship. But you'd be surprised how many use this argument.

Technically it is true that the word "adultery" refers to sex relations with a married person. Fornication means sex relations in the case of the unmarried. But the Bible makes it clear that both are wrong in God's sight. *Westminster Bible Dictionary,* which is one of the best, says this under "Fornication": "Illicit sexual intercourse on the part of an individual clearly violated the Seventh Commandment, set up to protect the permanency and sacredness of the family."

That last part is all-important. Always the saddest thing about doing wrong is that we missed the fun of doing right. One of my minister friends is fond of saying, "It's hell if you don't make heaven." That's how it is with sex. The self-made hell we get ourselves into isn't the worst part. The worst part is the heaven we miss.

Etcetera Number 26

"What Is Married Sex Like?"

What is married sex like? I don't mean how beautiful but some of the other things. I have read about how nice it is, but I am still wondering. How often do they do it? What all goes on when you are married?

Most parents would be surprised how often I get questions like this. I happen to believe that teenagers can handle sex best if they know what they want to know. So I will try to give you as complete answers as I can. Nobody can tell exactly what it will be like for you. You never know ahead of time how two people will react.

For example, take your question about how often. Some couples are happy with intercourse once a week. For others with more vigorous appetites this wouldn't be often enough. There are some marriages where it is a nice part of every day together. Happy couples care a lot about each other's needs. With them, trying to satisfy the mate is every bit as important as being satisfied.

It is also true that ways to do it are different with each couple. Some have a lot of fun thinking of themselves as "sexual athletes." They go for many different positions and unusual things. Others like it more subdued. They may prefer the slow, easy, quiet way. Some wouldn't think of sex any place but in their bedroom. Others enjoy making love wherever they feel a sense of safety and privacy.

Most marriage counselors today tell people: When you are married there is nothing wrong with anything you wish to do. You must understand, however, that this is true only under these two conditions: (1) That what you want to do is pleasing to you both. (2) That it is not physically or emotionally harmful to either of you.

You can see how all these things would take time. The greatest sex is not something that happens by chance. It has certain prerequisites which it demands. I mean like *total* involvement, *permanently*.

Christian couples will add this third qualification: anything forbidden in the Bible is wrong. However, the Bible speaks in different ways to different people. So I say it one more time: in some situations each couple must prayerfully work out their own answers with the Lord.

Epilogue

A Word to Fellow Parents

In tiny handwriting, scrawled on a postcard, comes this tribute from an irate mother to me:

Sir:
   I hate to think what is going to happen to you in the last days which are coming soon when we are all going to be judged at the judgment seat like the Scripture says. The government ought to protect us parents from people like you. But there is so much evil in Washington I don't suppose they will do anything. I don't want my daughter to know the awful things that go on today between all those juvenile delinquents. Don't worry about my Elizabeth. When she gets married, I will tell her all about her organs and what she is in for, and that will be soon enough.

Yours truly,

But I *do* have some concern for Elizabeth. The reason is that I know too many like her who need the very thing she's not getting.
   Let's face it—Our generation has done a sorry, sorry job of passing along sex as it ought to be delivered.
So the smut peddlers took over.
And the perverts paraded their sickness.

And the sexpots threw it around.
And they called it "freedom of expression."
And Elizabeth all this time was reading and gaping and listening and wondering . . . and she felt some strange stirrings . . . nice, but new and what do they mean?
And so did her girl friends! And here come the boy friends. And "What's new, baby?" . . . "Come on let's swing!" . . . "Get with it" . . . "Teach me tonight!"
And we? Adults?
 decrying and sighing and pointing our finger
And "Oh! isn't it awful?"

Some day, far off in the distance is it?
When the earth has cooled from the last big blowup,
Will there be a wise race of people who will understand sex?
What it really is and Holy?
 And fathers will sit with their daughters, won't they?
 And they will tell how a real man sees it.
 And mothers will walk with their sons, I think,
 And train their boys on women.
 And the family will be what it should be,
 Open, and honest, and fearless.
 And that will be the day
 When the whole world knows,
 Including the teenagers,
 That it is just as it says forever:
  "So God created man in his own image . . .
  male and female he created them . . .
  And God saw everything that he had made,
  and behold, it was very good."

 Yes! That will be the day!

About Charlie Shedd

Charlie Shedd is a full-time speaker/lecturer and writer—the best-selling author of numerous magazine articles and more than a dozen books (see list on the following pages). He and his wife, Martha, his coauthor on two books, travel nationwide, conducting their marriage seminar, Fun Marriage Forums. In addition, Charlie continues to write a nationally syndicated column, "Strictly for Dads," and he appears on a radio syndication called "Marriage Talk." Charlie and Martha Shedd have five grown children and five grandchildren.

Also by Charlie Shedd

For young people . . .
You Are Somebody Special (edited by Charlie Shedd)
How to Know If You're Really in Love

On marriage . . .
Letters to Karen: On Keeping Love in Marriage
Letters to Philip: On How to Treat a Woman
Talk to Me
The Best Dad Is a Good Lover
Celebration in the Bedroom (coauthored with Martha Shedd)
How to Stay in Love (coauthored with Martha Shedd)

For parents and grandparents . . .
You Can Be a Great Parent
Smart Dads I Know
A Dad Is for Spending Time With
Grandparents: Then God Created Grandparents and
    It Was Very Good
Grandparents' Family Book

To help you manage your life . . .
The Fat Is in Your Head
Time for All Things: Ten Affirmations for Christian Use of Time
Devotions for Dieters

Ideas for churches . . .
The Exciting Church: Where People Really Pray
The Exciting Church: Where They Give Their Money Away
The Exciting Church: Where They Really Use the Bible
The Pastoral Ministry of Church Officers

Cassette Resource Kits . . .
Fun Family Forum
Straight Talk on Love, Sex, and Marriage
Good Times with the Bible